A Note from the Editor

You are about to take a journey backward in time. Your means of transportation will be the written word and some glorious photographs. Your journey will take you, decade by decade, through the 20th century . . . our century.

Many of the events described in each issue of *Our Century* magazine are famous. Some have perhaps been forgotten. Many of the people were extraordinary, some merely ordinary, a few certainly evil. But all these events and people have one thing in common: they have made this century a fascinating and momentous one.

All of us who worked on *Our Century* hope you find your journey into the past interesting and educational. And most of all we hope you enjoy these "snapshots in time" as much as we enjoyed recapturing them for you.

Tony Napoli
Editor-in-Chief, *Our Century*

Statistics

	1930	1940
Population of the United States	123.1 million	131.7 million
Number of states in the United States	48	48
Number of cities with populations over 1 million	5	9
Population by race:		
White	110.3 million	118.2 million
Negro	11.9 million	12.8 million
Other	878,078	713,367
Population by sex:		
Male	62.2 million	66.1 million
Female	60.9 million	65.6 million
Population per square mile	41.2	44.2
Life expectancy in years:		
Male	58.1	60.8
Female	61.6	68.2
Three leading causes of death	Heart disease	Heart disease
	Influenza and pneumonia	Malignant tumors
	Malignant tumors	Influenza and pneumonia
Unemployment rate (14 and over)	8.7%	14.6%
Number of workers belonging to a union	3.6 million	8.1 million
Number of workers' strikes	637	2,508
Average hourly pay of worker in manufacturing plant	55¢	66¢
Illiteracy rate	4.3%	2.9%
School enrollment (public/secondary)	4,399,000	6,601,000
Percent of all 17 year olds who graduated from high school	49%	28.8%
College degrees—Bachelors:		
Male	73,600	109,000
Female	48,800	77,000
Number of lynchings	21	5
Attendance at movies (weekly)	90 million	80 million
Attendance at baseball games (yearly)	10.2 million	10 million
Prices:		
dozen eggs	44¢	33¢
quart of milk	14¢	13¢
loaf of bread	9¢	8¢
pound of butter	46¢	36¢
pound of coffee	39¢	21¢
dozen oranges	57¢	29¢

OUR CENTURY

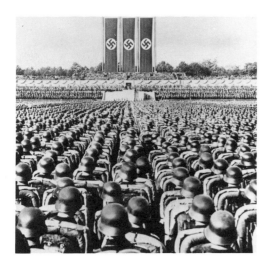
By Marna Owen
Designer: Detta Penna

All photographs: The Bettmann Archive, with the following exceptions: pp. 5-7, 45, 47 (bottom): National
Archives; pp. 14-17, 24, 52, 55, 59: UPI/Bettmann Newsphotos; p. 49: Library of Congress. Advertise-
ments on endpapers: The D'Arcy Collection, University of Illinois at Urbana-Champaign.
"End O' My Line" (page 47), words and new music adaptation by Woody Guthrie. TRO © 1963 Ludlow
Music, Inc. New York, N.Y. Reprinted by permission.

1930–1940

Please visit our web site at: www.garethstevens.com
For a free color catalog describing Gareth Stevens' list of high-quality books and multimedia programs,
call 1-800-542-2595 (USA) or 1-800-461-9120 (Canada). Gareth Stevens Publishing's Fax: (414) 332-3567.

Library of Congress Cataloging-in-Publication Data

Our century.
    p. cm.
    Originally published: Belmont, Calif.: Fearon Education, 1989.
    Includes bibliographical references and index.
    Contents: [1] 1900-1910/written by Janice Greene — [2] 1910-1920/written by Karen Liberatore — [3] 1920-1930/written by Prescott Hill — [4] 1930-1940/
written by Marna Owen — [5] 1940-1950/written by Prescott Hill — [6] 1950-1960/written by S. D. Jones — [7] 1960-1970/written by Joyce Lane —
[8] 1970-1980/written by Prescott Hill — [9] 1980-1990/written by Joanne Suter.
    ISBN 0-8368-1035-X [4] (lib. bdg.)
    1. Civilization, Modern—20th century—Juvenile literature. [1. History, Modern—20th century. 2. Civilization, Modern—20th century.]
CB425.O97 1993
909.82—dc20   93-11445

This North American edition published by
Gareth Stevens Publishing
A World Almanac Education Group Company
330 West Olive Street, Suite 100
Milwaukee, WI 53212 USA

This edition first published in 1993 by Gareth Stevens, Inc. Originally published in 1989 by Fearon Education, 500 Harbor Boulevard,
Belmont, California, 94002, with © 1989 by Fearon Education. End matter © 1993 by Gareth Stevens, Inc.

Printed in the United States of America

6 7 8 9 10 11 12 05 04 03 02 01

Gareth Stevens Publishing
A WORLD ALMANAC EDUCATION GROUP COMPANY

Education

Enrollments Are Up, Job Prospects Uncertain

The 1930s were a tough time for young people in America. School, adults told them, was the place to be. Without an education, the future would be dark. But the depression years guaranteed no one a job. It didn't seem to matter how bright a person was, or how many years of school someone had. In 1933 one-third of all college graduates could not find work. A popular tune among college students was:

> I sing in praise of college,
> Of M.A.'s and Ph.D.'s
> But in pursuit of knowledge
> We are starving by degrees.

Yet, the 1930s saw more and more young people starting high school than ever before. In 1920 about 28% of all youngsters of high school age were in school. By 1930 this number was 47%. And at the end of the decade, 80% of the high school age population was enrolled.

What was the reason for this high percentage? Many believe that young people simply had few choices. Since there were no jobs, school or the streets were the only places they had to spend time.

And many young people did choose the streets over school. In 1934 four million youths, ages 16–24, were neither employed nor in school. A 1939 study shocked the country. It found that 90% of all people being held for major crimes were under the age of 30. American youth had

found that if jobs wouldn't pay, crime would.

But schools did their best to teach good citizenship anyway. By 1935 all students had to take classes on the state and federal constitutions.

Yet, it was hard for students to believe in their government when it seemed that little was being done to help educate them. While President Roosevelt spent nine billion dollars on work programs, few of these dollars went for better education. Young men who joined the Civilian Conservation Corps did study in camp. But most learned forestry skills which didn't help them get a job when the Corps ended. The National Youth Administration gave some money to high school and college students as encouragement to stay in school. But to many the future still looked bleak.

> Some American youths found that if jobs wouldn't pay, crime would.

Some college students of the 1930s lost faith in the democratic form of government. Many became involved in student groups run by the Young Communist League. They believed that the Soviet Union's communist government was a model for sharing a country's wealth.

Other college groups campaigned actively for world peace in the 1930s. On April 13, 1933 there was a nationwide Student Strike Against War. More than 25,000 students took part. A national poll showed that 39% of young men in the United States said they would not fight in any war. Another 33% said that they would fight only if the United States were attacked by another country. This unpatriotic news shocked a nation of adults who had fought in the Great War. The familiar question, "What is happening to our young people?" was heard across the land. ∎

"What is happening to our young people?"

Many students in the country still learned the "three Rs" in close quarters. At the beginning of the decade there were still 150,000 one-room schoolhouses in the United States.

This grateful worker is one of the many lucky people who found work through the Works Progress Administration (WPA).

Employment

Hard Times for American Workers

A man is arrested in Brooklyn, New York, for sleeping on a cot in a vacant lot. He tells the judge about his life. He is an engineer and 44 years old. He's worked in the United States, China, Panama, and Venezuela. He doesn't want to be sleeping on that cot. He just can't find a job.

That man's story tells it all. In the spring of 1930, the United States had 4 million unemployed workers.

By 1932 the number had skyrocketed to 15 million. There were no jobs for one-fourth of America's workers.

Unemployment hit just about everybody. Four-fifths of all steel mills closed, leaving factory workers on the streets. Farmers lost their livelihood when they could not get good prices for their surplus crops and meats. The price of cotton went from 30 cents a pound to 6 cents a pound. During the 1930s, farm earnings

dropped by two-thirds from what they had been in 1929. In 1935 over 200,000 teachers could not find work. Even doctors lost money. As a group, their earnings dropped by 40%.

Perhaps hardest hit were young Americans. In 1935 almost three million—or one-third of all young people—were out of work.

People tried to make money in any way they could. Once the American Shippers Association found itself with an unsellable load of apples. What happened? The Association gave the apples to the unemployed on credit. The street corners of New York City were soon crowded with 6,000 apple sellers.

The Government Puts America to Work

President Franklin Roosevelt, elected in 1932, tried to put America to work with government money. The Civilian Conservation Corps employed 250,000 young men. For $1 a day plus room and board, they planted trees and worked on America's parklands. The Federal Emergency Relief Act gave $500 million dollars to the states. Each state used the money in its own work programs.

The Civil Works Administration put unemployed Americans to work in a number of ways. They built 40,000 schools in which 50,000 teachers found work. Lonely country roads were paved; 500 airports were built. Artists found work in the Public Works Art Project (PWA), and later in the Works Progress Administration (WPA). In its first five months, the PWA paid 4,000 artists for their paintings and crafts. Murals were painted in many federal and state government buildings. Often the murals showed workers of the 1930s, trying to scrape out a living.

All told, the federal government spent $9 billion dollars on work programs. Yet, in 1938, there were still 9 million people unemployed. ∎

Labor Laws

Roosevelt tried to improve labor conditions with the National Industrial Recovery Act. Under its codes, workers earned a minimum of $15 a week. And they could only be made to work 40 hours. Child labor was outlawed. Workers were guaranteed the right to bargain for better pay and working conditions. Because of this new right, workers' strikes were up by one-third in 1933.

Still, many workers were glad to get what they could. Take the case of farmers in the Dust Bowl. They were driven from the Plains states in the mid-1930s by dust storms and drought. (See story, page 44.) Many were happy to work on California farms for $1 a day or less.

During the decade, about one-quarter of the population still lived, and made their livings, on farms.

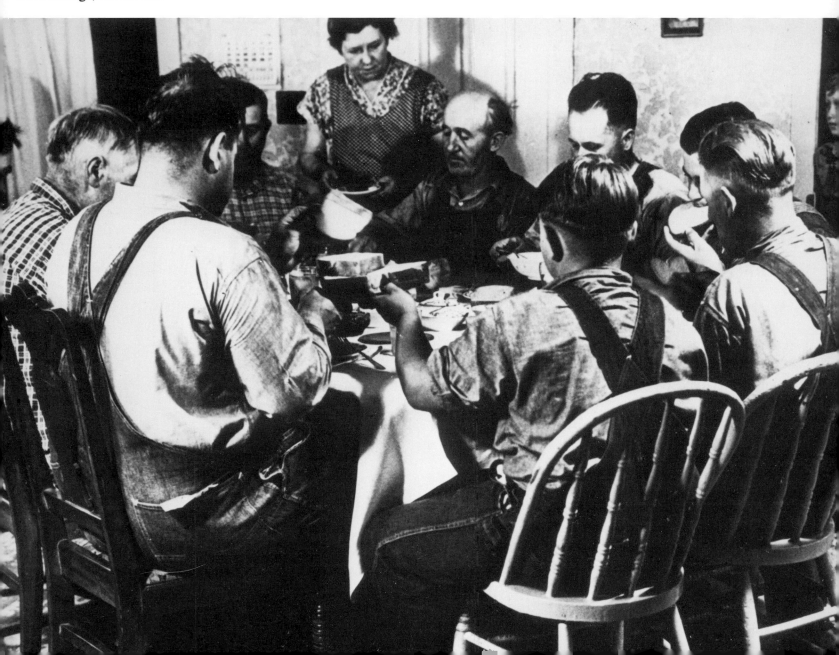

Fashion

The Knees Disappear— New Styles More Elegant

The world was shocked when women's knees popped into the fashion scene in the 1920s. Flappers flirted with short skirts; women's hair was cut short, too. But the 1930s brought a more elegant look into style. Dresses for daytime wear dropped below the knee, almost to the ankle. Evening dresses touched the floor, making graceful sweeps across ballroom floors. The more glitter on those evening dresses, the better. Women began to grow their hair, waving it into soft curls.

While knees disappeared, women's waistlines reappeared. No more of those drop-waisted dresses of the 1920s. Fitted suits and belted dresses showed a woman's curves in the 1930s. The best-dressed women of the decade wore fur-trimmed jackets. For evening, only a full length fox or mink would do.

And to top it off: the hat. It was unthinkable that any woman would step outdoors without one. The photo on this page shows the decade's bolder hat styles (from Paris, of course). Hats were tipped slightly to one side. High heels and leather bags completed the smart look.

Men also had their special "look" in this decade. For evening, nothing would do but a tuxedo. But what about those more casual moments? Something new crashed the American men's fashion scene in 1936. It was the Jippa Jappa, or "Yippee," from the Bahamas. This light straw hat

Hats were the icing on the cake in fashion during the 1930s. These stunning styles came from Paris.

8

This gentleman is wearing the latest in tuxedos.

A smart, fitted suit was very popular for women's day wear.

kept the sun off many a well-groomed head. For walking, men wore lightweight rubber-soled shoes called Skokies. And every man needed a silk scarf, pipe, and leather briefcase, as well as the ever-present hat.

Men dressed just as well on vacation. Men's pirate striped shirts turned the beaches into rows of candy stripes. (It is said that two Greeks had forgotten their beach shirts on a trip to the French Riviera. Instead, they wore their striped pajama tops. Voila! A new fashion was born.) And for show, men tied their beach trunks with very colorful silk scarves. Who says women always have all the fashion fun in the fashion world? ■

Men wear striped shirts on the beach.

Spain in the 1930s

A Decade of Division, Destruction, and Death

"We are out of fashion," the king sadly told his friends before leaving Spain.

It will be remembered as a time of brother against brother, a time of blood and bombs. This is the story of Spain during the 1930s. A decade that began with the bright promise of democracy, but ended in the bitter despair of dictatorship.

In 1931 Spain was a discouraged country. Once a great empire, it had lost its last American and Asian colonies in the Spanish-American War of 1898. The country's 25 million people were ruled by a small group of rich and powerful people: King Alfonso XIII, his royal friends, the leaders of the Catholic Church, and landowners.

It was in the fields of these landowners that most Spanish workers made a living. They raised cattle or grew olives and grapes. And many Spanish workers toiled long hours in factories which were years behind most factories in Europe and America. The pay for a long day's work in a factory or under the hot Spanish sun was twelve to forty cents. And the Spanish people were tired of it.

On April 12, 1931, the majority of Spanish people voted against the king and for the new Republic. In the Republic, the people would rule themselves by voting for government representatives. The leaders of the Republic said they would divide land equally among the Spanish people. The result would be more freedom, and a better life for all.

But after the elections there was trouble in the air. The rich landowners and the church leaders were afraid of the Republic. They wanted their king back, and they were ready to fight. But King Alfonso knew when he was beaten. And he did not want to see the people of his country fighting against one another. He decided to leave the country, a country his family had ruled for hundreds of years. "We are out of fashion," he sadly told his friends before leaving Spain.

With the king gone, many Spaniards felt full of hope. The people called the new government *la niña bonita*, the pretty girl.

The new Republic set about making changes. For hundreds of years, the Catholic religion had been Spain's official religion. A new constitution called for the separation of church and government. The new constitution also gave women the right to vote. And it guaranteed other freedoms and rights to all people of Spain. Laws were passed to help equally divide land among the poor.

Yet, with all these good ideas,

Spain became more disorderly and troubled. Catholic churches were burned across the countryside. In the south, the rich landowners refused to give up their land. And they refused to plant crops. The poor workers became hungrier than ever, and they began to doubt the Republic.

A group of people called anarchists also caused trouble for the Republic. The anarchists wanted the country to be run without any government at all. They wanted no king, army, landlords, bosses, priests, or nuns. They believed that all should share in the country's land, factories, and wealth.

To accomplish their goals, the anarchists led worker strikes. In July 1931 they tried to take over the government of the city of Seville. This attempt ended in bloodshed, with the government troops killing 30 and wounding 200. It seemed the "pretty girl Republic" was turning ugly. ■

In 1931 King Alfonso XIII voluntarily left Spain to make way for a new government.

Spanish Nationalist forces shell Republican positions outside Madrid in November 1936.

Trouble in Spain Escalates
Civil War Breaks Out

In 1933 the Spanish people called for a change. They elected CEDA into power. CEDA was a Catholic group. Once in power, it began to return Spain to its old ways. Landowners paid workers less. Rents went up. Factory workers were fired.

The Spanish voters who had elected CEDA to power were outraged. These were not the changes they had hoped for. Soon trouble spread through the streets. In 1934 workers in a small mining area called Asturias revolted. They united and

declared themselves free from the Spanish government. General Francisco Franco and the Spanish army joined forces to bring the Asturias miners to their knees. The miners surrendered. But to Franco and the CEDA government, this was not enough. The miners were tortured, put in prison, or killed.

Power again changed hands in the elections of 1936. The new leaders of the Republic freed the Asturias prisoners. Land was divided among the poor. General Franco and other powerful army leaders were sent to an island out of the country. There it would be harder for them to interfere with the new government. But as the world now knows, Franco was not stopped.

It was Franco who finally led a rebellion against the Republican government. Under his leadership, the Spanish army gained new power. On July 17, 1936, army units stationed in Morocco, in Africa, took over Spanish buildings and the radio station there.

The people of Barcelona wave posters of General Franco as they welcome Nationalist forces to the city.

"It is better to die on your feet than to live on your knees!"

People who sided with the Republic were captured or shot. Back in Spain, a Madrid radio broadcaster nicknamed *La Pasionaria* (the passionate one) called to her listeners to fight Franco's army. "It is better to die on your feet than to live on your knees!" she cried. Spain was fighting Spain. The Civil War had begun.

Franco's followers became known as the Nationalists. The Nationalists wanted a fascist government in Spain. All Spanish businesses would work for this government. All Spanish people would be expected to do whatever the government asked. The Nationalists wanted to return power to the Church, the army, and the wealthy. The fascist countries of Italy and Germany were glad to help. They sent airplanes, bombs, guns, and men to assist the Spanish Nationalists.

More than 100,000 Italians and 15,000 Germans joined the fight.

Those who still believed in the Republic were called Loyalists. The Loyalists were made up of communists, anarchists, and many workers who had hoped for a free and fair Spain. The Loyalists had a smaller, less prepared army than their opponents. Help came to them from the Soviet Union, a communist country. The Soviets sent some food, weapons, and men to aid the Loyalists. And from more than 50 countries, volunteer soldiers, known as the International Brigades, came to fight against a fascist Spain. (See story on page 16).

Many Prisoners Murdered

Right from the beginning, it was a terrible war. Both sides were destructive and cruel in the name of their cause. Early in the war, the Loyalists rounded up 2,000 Nationalists from Madrid jails. These prisoners were taken to nearby villages and shot. Catholic priests were also executed by the Loyalists. But the Nationalists were just as bad. They murdered 1,800 Loyalists in a bullring—gunning them down for twelve hours with machine guns. Blood stains covered the once peaceful fields of Spain. ■

Franco's forces were better armed than the poor Republican army. Here they use machine guns to mow down Republican soldiers.

Madrid was the last stronghold of the Republican army. The city fell to Franco's forces on March 27, 1939.

The Final Battle: Madrid

Throughout 1937 and 1938, the Nationalists captured one city after another: Málaga, Bilbao, Teruel, Vinaroz. And then in January 1939 Franco took Barcelona, one of the last major areas of Loyalist resistance. Now only Madrid, the capital city, remained.

For many Spaniards, Madrid was *the* symbol of the Loyalist cause. The Loyalists had denied the rebels an early victory in the war in 1936. The Loyalists battle cry had been: *No pasaran* ("They shall not pass."). And for nearly three years that promise was kept as the Nationalists were repelled time and time again.

But now, in March 1939, Franco's forces held a death grip on Madrid. As the Nationalists closed in, the Loyalists crumbled. Fighting broke out between the communists and anticommunists within the Loyalist movement. Many of the anticommunists hoped if they changed sides, the Nationalists would show mercy when the city finally fell. Their actions only hastened the end. With Loyalist troops near exhaustion from fighting one another, Franco's armies marched, practically unopposed, into Madrid on March 29. After almost three bitter years of fighting, and more than 700,000 deaths, Spain's Civil War had ended. ∎

Spain's New Leader: General Francisco Franco

When the Nationalist forces captured Madrid, General Francisco Franco became the military dictator of Spain. An army officer since the age of 20, Franco had risen quickly through the ranks to become a general by the age of 34. By the time the Nationalists revolted against the government, Franco had established his reputation as the leader of Spain's army.

Franco had made it clear many times during the Civil War that he thought it was a battle to the death. His only goal was unconditional surrender by the Loyalists. He felt no remorse about ridding Spain of anyone he considered an enemy. If he needed to be ruthless and merciless to overthrow the Republic, he was certainly up to the task. Said one man who served under him in the Spanish Foreign Legion in Morocco: "I've seen murderers go white in the face because Franco looked at them out of the corner of his eyes. You know the man's not quite human, and he hasn't got any nerves."

What angered Franco most about the Republic was the disorder of Spanish life. He and his supporters were deeply offended by the demands of the lower classes for a better, freer life. Those in the Army particularly felt that the rapid changes, and the strikes, the riots, and protests in the early 1930s had brought much dishonor to Spain. Franco's solution to the problem was a military one. Death to the enemy—in battle and after battle—was his way of imposing order and restoring the country's honor. ■

General Francisco Franco

Side-by-Side With the Spanish Loyalists

> "You can go with pride. You are legend . . . we will not forget you."

Men and women from America, England, France—from more than 50 countries in all—came to help the Loyalists. They were called the International Brigades. Few had training as soldiers. Yet they fought side by side with the Spanish Loyalists under terrible conditions. Sometimes they had only rats to eat, and often they couldn't wash for months at a time. Why did they come? Why did they choose to stay?

The International Brigades came to take a stand against Fascism. Their own countries refused to take a stand, or to help, in the war. So they felt they had to do it on their own.

Though the Brigade soldiers were relatively few in number (around 40,000) and untrained, they did bring hope to the Loyalists when things seemed darkest. Without them, the Loyalists could not have kept Franco out of Madrid for as long as they did.

Most of the Brigades left Spain by the autumn of 1938. The last of them paraded through Barcelona's wide streets. Tearful Spaniards cheered and called their goodbyes. *La Pasionaria* made a moving farewell speech. "You can go with pride. You are history. You are legend . . . we will not forget you. (When the Republic wins) Come back to us and here you will find a homeland." ∎

The Lincoln Brigade helped fight the fascist forces in the Spanish Civil War. Here, wounded members of the American force have returned to New York.

Wallis Warfield Simpson and the former King of England. They are now known as the Duchess and Duke of Windsor.

To Marry the Woman He Loves . . .

The King Steps Down

January 1936 was a sad time in England. King George V was dead. All of England mourned his loss. During the funeral, the royal crown was placed on the dead king's coffin. People watched in horror as the jeweled cross fell off the crown. It was an omen, people said. It was a sign of bad things to come.

On December 11, 1936, the shocked nation saw that "bad thing" come to pass. The new king, Edward VIII, gave up the crown. He said he could not rule as king of England. His reason for abdicating? He wanted to marry a divorced woman. She was Wallis Warfield Simpson, a twice-divorced American woman from Baltimore.

Their romance had been no secret. In fact, the couple had started keeping company before Wallis's second divorce. Edward, then the Prince of Wales, had invited Wallis and her husband, Ernest, to Fort Belvedere four years earlier in 1932. It wasn't long before the Prince was calling on Wallis at her own home.

At first it seemed to be nothing more than friendship. But in time, Wallis and the young prince were seen together far too often without her husband. When she divorced Ernest in October 1936, the stories began to fly.

Although she is not known for her beauty, it is said that men have always been strongly attracted to Mrs. Simpson. And those who saw the king and Wallis together could easily see the power she held over him.

King Edward was determined to make Wallis his wife. But the rest of England didn't think the divorced American would be a proper queen for their country. So Edward's ministers gave him two choices. They said he could either forget about marrying Mrs. Simpson, or abdicate the throne and marry her.

To Edward there was no choice. And when friends of the king asked Mrs. Simpson to leave the country, she explained that it wouldn't solve the problem. "You don't understand. He would simply follow me."

After the abdication, Edward's brother, who became George VI, succeeded to the throne. Edward was given the title of Duke of Windsor. And with their wedding in June 1937, Wallis Simpson became the Duchess of Windsor. ■

The Nazis Rise to Power

A lock of dark hair falls across his forehead. The look on his face is intense. People who meet him argue about the color of his eyes. Are they blue-grey or a greenish brown?

When Adolf Hitler speaks in front of crowds as head of the Nazi party, the applause is deafening. The message is just what the people want to hear. The Nazi party, he says is for ". . . peace, work, bread, honor, and justice." On January 30, 1933, the man is named Chancellor of Germany. Only then does the world begin the see what Adolf Hitler means by "peace, honor, and justice."

Hitler's first act is to call for new elections. He wants his Nazi party to win the majority of seats in the Reichstag, or German Parliament. When it looks as though his party will not win, he orders the Nazis to set the Reichstag building on fire. The German people do not know it, but their whole country is being set ablaze.

Hitler blames the fire on German Communists. He urges the aging president of Germany, Paul von Hindenburg, to take away the rights of the Communists. It is no coincidence that many of the Communists are Jews. Hindenburg agrees. What follows is a tragedy: More than 4,000 Communist leaders are rounded up, beaten, and tortured by Hitler's Nazis. Many are sent away to concentration camps. And surprisingly enough, Hitler's actions have the backing of most of the German people.

How did such a man come to power? The answer goes back to the end of the Great War. The Treaty of Versailles, signed in 1919, formally ended the fighting among European countries. Most of Europe was relieved, but Germany was furious. The treaty took away Germany's colonies. It demanded that Germany pay war debts to France and Great Britain. And it forced Germany to give up part of its land to Poland and the Allies. The Treaty of Versailles was a daily reminder to Germans that they had lost the war. They carried this shame with them through the coming decade.

The 1920s were hard times for Germany in other ways as well. Inflation was at an all-time high. The story was told about a woman who sold her furniture to buy a postage stamp. And postwar Germany was a hard place to make a living.

It was Adolf Hitler who promised to make Germany strong again. During the 1920s, he spoke of his

Thousands of German troops gather in Nuremberg for a rally and a speech by Nazi leader Adolf Hitler.

dream to huge crowds of people. He made a lot of promises. He would strike down the Treaty of Versailles. Germany's armed forces would be made strong again under his leadership. Germans would take back the land their country had lost in the war. And they would wipe out the Communist Soviet Union, Germany's enemy.

An Early Power Grab

Back in 1923 Hitler had tried to seize power. He led 3,000 workers into the streets of Munich. Their goal was to overthrow the German government. For this, Hitler was arrested and sent to prison. While there, he wrote *Mein Kampf (My Struggle),* a book that outlined his beliefs. In it he said that the Jews had contaminated the true German people, which he called the Aryan race. Once the Jews were out of the way, he said, the Aryan race would become strong. Someday, it would rule the world.

Hitler spent only nine months in jail. When he got out, he continued to spread his ideas through his newly named National Socialist Workers Party, or Nazis. The tired and proud German people began to listen to Hitler's dreams. The Jews, who were only one percent of the German population, had little to say about the Nazis coming to power. And as Hitler's dreams came true, so did the worst nightmares of the German Jews. ■

> The tired and proud German people began to listen to Hitler's dreams.

Hitler inspects his troops in a military parade in Berlin.

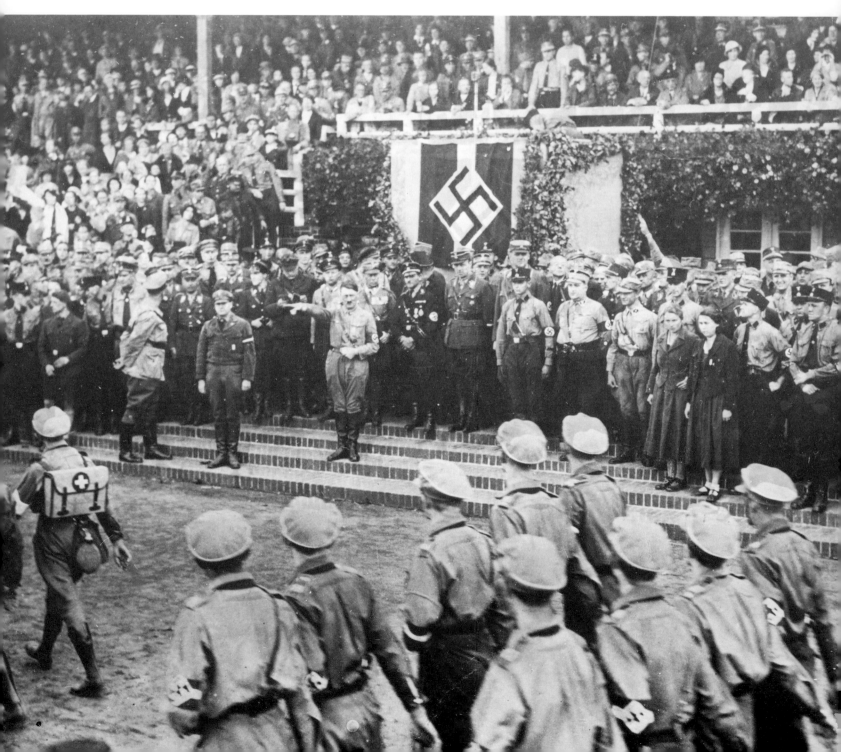

The Nazis began a boycott of Jewish stores in 1933. The signs read: "Germans, be on your guard. Don't buy from Jews."

Hitler Lashes Out at the Jews

Hitler moved quickly to take total power in Germany. First he pushed through the Enabling Act. This act gave him the power to pass laws and give orders without talking to the Reichstag. Then in 1934, President von Hindenburg died. This gave Hitler the chance to make himself the Führer, the supreme head of Germany. Now, nothing stood in his way.

He began to build up Germany's armed forces. Enough tanks, guns, and submarines were manufactured to take over all of Europe. And he waged a war against the Jews.

The war began with the Nuremberg laws passed in 1935. These laws took away the citizenship of Jews—

they were now "subjects." No longer were Jews and Germans allowed to marry or do business with one another. And Jewish books were burned.

In 1938 a 17-year-old Jewish boy in Paris decided he'd had enough of Hitler. His parents had just sent him a letter. It read, "Tonight it was announced that Polish Jews are being expelled from Germany. At 9 o'clock the police arrived and took us to the police station. They are going to expel us from Germany and make us go back to Poland. What shall we do there, my son? . . . Thank God you are safe in France."

The boy took his parents' letter

to heart. He walked to the German embassy in Paris and asked to see a person of high rank. He had secrets to share, he said. The boy was shown to the desk of German Ernst Von Rath. Rath looked up from his desk. The young boy took out a gun and shot at Rath five times. Two bullets hit the mark. "I had to make my feelings clear," he later told police.

The young boy's action was felt as far away as Germany. Nazi leaders decided it was time to teach the Jews a good lesson.

Kristallnacht

The *Gestapo* (government police) sent notices to state and local police officials on November 9, 1938. The notices said there would be widespread demonstrations against the Jews. Plans had been made to arrest 20,000–30,000 Jews—about 5,000 in Austria alone.

Police were to allow the burning of Jewish synagogues as long as they were sure neighborhoods would not catch fire. Jewish homes and businesses could also be destroyed.

On the night of November 9, German soldiers dressed in regular clothes. They went into the streets. "Down with the dirty Jews!" they cried. They began to smash the windows of Jewish-owned stores. It didn't take the German people long to join in. Two nights of terror followed for the Jews.

Stores were broken into and picked clean by mobs of people. Jewish men were dragged into the streets and stripped of their clothing. Jewish women were raped. Houses, shops, and synagogues were burned. Thousands were arrested and sent to concentration camps. The event became known as *Kristallnacht*, the Night of Broken Glass.

On the morning of November 11, German cities were in ruins. Buildings smoked and broken glass was everywhere. Many German people walked with their heads down, as if ashamed.

But Hitler's men were proud. They had done their job well. Jews everywhere feared for their lives. Many of them began to flee the country. But for the ones unable to leave, life inside Germany became an increasing vision of hell. ∎

By 1938 the Nazis had arrested thousands of German Jews and sent them to concentration camps.

Europe's Leaders Sell Out Czechs at Munich

No one knew what Hitler would do next. In fact, his three so-called "Saturday surprises" had the countries of Europe worrying about their own safety.

The first Saturday surprise came on October 14, 1933. On that day, Hitler withdrew Germany from the League of Nations. The League, started after the Great War, was designed to work out problems between countries. Clearly, Hitler wanted no one to tell him what to do.

The second Saturday surprise came on March 16, 1935. On that date Hitler announced that the German draft for armed forces would begin. It could only mean that he was getting ready for war.

On March 7, 1936, Hitler shocked the world with his third Saturday surprise. German armies marched into the Rhineland, a territory of Western Germany near the French border. Since 1920, the Treaty of Versailles had barred soldiers from the Rhineland. But Hitler just marched in and took the land back. It was German land, he said. He could do what he wished with it.

France and Great Britain did nothing to stop him. Hitler, pleased with his victory, did not stop there.

In 1936 he had told the world he had no plans to take over his homeland of Austria. But little by little, he let the Austrian leaders know that German troops were ready to cross Austria's borders. In 1938 Austria's President Miklas gave in to Hitler's demands. He ordered Chancellor Kurt Schuschnigg out of the country. A Nazi government would be put in his place. Said Schuschnigg as he left the country, "So, I take leave of the

Leaders from Europe's most powerful countries met at Munich in 1938 to decide Czechoslovakia's fate. Left to right, Great Britain's Neville Chamberlain, France's Édouard Daladier, Germany's Adolf Hitler, and Italy's Benito Mussolini.

Austrian people with the German words of farewell uttered from the depths of my heart—God protect Austria."

When Hitler's troops marched in, Austria and Germany became one.

Hitler then set his eyes on Czechoslovakia. The Sudetenland of Czechoslovakia, he told Europe, really belonged to Germany. Now he wanted it back.

By this time, Great Britain and France were worried about war. If Hitler attacked democratic Czechoslovakia, they would have to fight. But Britain's Prime Minister Neville Chamberlain decided that war must be avoided at all costs. The price was Czechoslovakia.

In the fall of 1938, Europe's leaders met Hitler at Munich. No one from the Czechoslovakian government was present. The fate of that country was in the hands of Italy's Benito Mussolini, France's Édouard Daladier, and Britain's Neville Chamberlain.

On September 29, those present signed the Munich Pact. The Pact took away one-third of Czechoslovakia's land and population. Germany annexed 10,000 square miles and 3.5 million people. Hungary and Poland, which had also issued claims for Czech territory, were given

several thousand square miles.

The hearts and dreams of Czechoslovakians broke that day. The night before, Thomas Masaryk, one of the nation's founders, had died. President Eduard Benes felt betrayed by the democracies of Great Britain and France. He fled to the United States.

Chamberlain told Great Britain he had brought . . . "peace with honor" to Europe.

Chamberlain returned to his country with high hopes. He told Great Britain that he had brought ". . . peace with honor" to Europe. But his countryman Winston Churchill did not agree. "Do not suppose that this is the end," he said.

Meanwhile, German troops marched into the Czech Sudetenland. Hitler was pleased with another easy kill. He told the world: "This is the last territorial claim I have to make in Europe."

As the world soon learned, Hitler was lying. Six months later, he took over the rest of Czechoslovakia. ∎

After the "Munich sellout," German troops were free to take the Sudetenland from Czechoslovakia in October 1938.

Soviet Foreign Minister Vyacheslav Molotov signs Soviet-German Non-aggression Pact that carved up Poland for the two countries. Soviet Leader Josef Stalin (right) and German Foreign Minister Joachim Von Ribbentrop are all smiles about the agreement.

Stalin and Hitler
An Unholy Alliance

In 1938 Hitler went to the Polish government. He wanted the city of Danzig, once German, returned to his rule. He also wanted a strip of land called the Polish Corridor. On it he would build German highways and railroads. This would give Germany a new route to the sea.

But Polish leaders would not give in. They refused his request again and again. Hitler's anger grew by the day. One way or another he decided, Poland would be his.

Meanwhile Josef Stalin had been making his own plans. As leader of the Communist Soviet Union, he was certain that Hitler would someday attack his country. Many times Hitler had named the Soviet Union as his

worst enemy. But Stalin's army was not ready for a fight. He needed to buy some time.

Soviet Foreign Minister Vyacheslav Molotov began talks with Germany. Then on August 24, 1939, the announcement came. The Soviet Union and Germany had signed a Nonaggression Pact. This meant that they had agreed not to attack one another. Hitler was now free to take Poland if he wished. The Soviet Union would not come to Poland's aid. And Stalin felt the Soviet Union would now have the time it needed to build up its own forces.

Back in the United States, people could smell war. "If France and England go to war against

Germany, do you think the United States can stay out?" was the question asked in a 1939 poll. "No" was the answer given by 43% of the population.

Operation Canned Goods

It was summer, 1939. Thirteen German prisoners ate their last meal: soup, bread, a glass of beer, and a special treat of canned meat. So began Hitler's Operation Canned Goods.

The German prisoners, dressed in Polish uniforms, were taken to the Polish border. One by one, a deadly drug was injected into their arms. Unconscious, they were taken into Poland and propped up against trees facing Germany. The German soldiers smiled at their good work. It looked as though Poland was ready to attack Germany. This gave the German army just the excuse it needed.

In the early morning hours of September 1, 1939, Hitler's tanks and seven divisions of the German army stormed the Polish border. A German battleship entered Danzig harbor. After twelve hours of nonstop bombing, the people of Danzig surrendered.

On September 2, Hitler ordered an air raid on Warsaw. It was not just the Polish army that was to be hit. Homes, schools, and hospitals—all were German targets. At the same time, the Soviet Union attacked Poland from the east. The Soviets wanted part of this helpless country, too.

On September 3 at 9:00 A.M., Neville Chamberlain sent a message to Hitler. The message warned that if Germany did not take its army out of Poland by 11:00 A.M., Great Britain would go to war. The next two hours passed slowly. At 11:13 A.M., Chamberlain rose slowly from his chair. Before he made his announcement of war, he spoke quietly to a friend. "This is a sad day for all of us, and to none is it sadder than me."

At 5:00 P.M. that day France also declared war on Germany. For the second time in this century, Europe was at war. ■

Back in the United States, people could smell war.

German troops invaded Poland on September 1, 1939. The following day Europe was at war.

Out of Work, Out of Food, Out of Luck

Hundreds of unemployed people line up for food rations along New York's famous Times Square.

Remember New Year's Day, 1930? The 369th Infantry Band, made up of thirty Negroes, played lively music on the floor of the New York Stock Exchange. People danced and sang. Everyone seemed to enjoy the fine party. Looking back, there was little cause for celebration.

As it turned out, Americans were fooling themselves. In 1930 they were counting on another ten years filled with plenty of money and good times. They were unable to see what was really coming: the Great Depression, years of hunger, of sadness, of unemployment and homelessness.

The trouble began with the stock market crash of October 1929. It came as quite a shock. In the 1920s businesses, banks, working men with little money, and even housewives had bought shares of stocks. All believed the prices of the stocks would continue to go up. When the time came to sell the stock, they would become rich. And many people *did* make money in the 1920s. But the system fell apart when everybody tried to sell at once. The stock prices fell. And those who had dreamed of becoming rich were left penniless.

But that was just the beginning. Many of the banks and businesses that lost money in the stock market had to close. This forced people out of work. Without jobs, people had little or no money to spend on American goods. As spending dropped, more businesses lost money and closed. Banks found it impossible to collect on loans. How could they collect money that people didn't have? As businesses and banks closed their doors, the streets became crowded with the homeless and the jobless.

The subway was the cheapest "hotel" for New York's jobless.

What was it like to live in America in the Depression years? The experiences of those living in New York City, with some variation, could apply almost anywhere else as well. Most job seekers found it useless to go to job agencies. The agencies wanted $10 up front just to get a man a job. Often the jobs lasted just a few days. And wages were only around three or four dollars a day. ⇨

The cheapest "hotel" for the jobless in New York City was the subway train from Times Square to Coney Island. Hundreds rode this route, sleeping in a fairly comfortable seat for the two-hour ride. In Grand Central Station a person could wash up for five cents. As for food, well . . . there were always the breadlines. They stretched for blocks. And a good meal of soup, bread, and maybe coffee could be had after hours and hours of waiting. People talked happily after they had eaten. For the moment, many seemed to believe they would find work the next day. Then the moment passed and they were back on the streets.

If you were a Negro looking for work, things were even worse. The jobless rate among Negroes was often six times higher than it was among whites. Whites were given jobs before Negroes. And Negroes were fired and replaced by whites. The desperate situation drove Negro and white Americans farther and farther apart, adding to the tension in the air.

And those who did find work? In 1932, New York City had 7,000 people shining shoes for a living. In Chicago, factory girls were paid 25 cents an hour. Even the great baseball star Babe Ruth took a $10,000 cut in yearly pay. ∎

Cold Hard Facts of the Great Depression

Between 1930 and 1933:

- Stock prices went down 80%.

- 9,000 banks went out of business.

- 9 million savings accounts were wiped out.

- 86,000 businesses failed.

- The percent of jobless people in the population went from 9% to 25% (15 million people).

- Wages fell by an average of 60%.

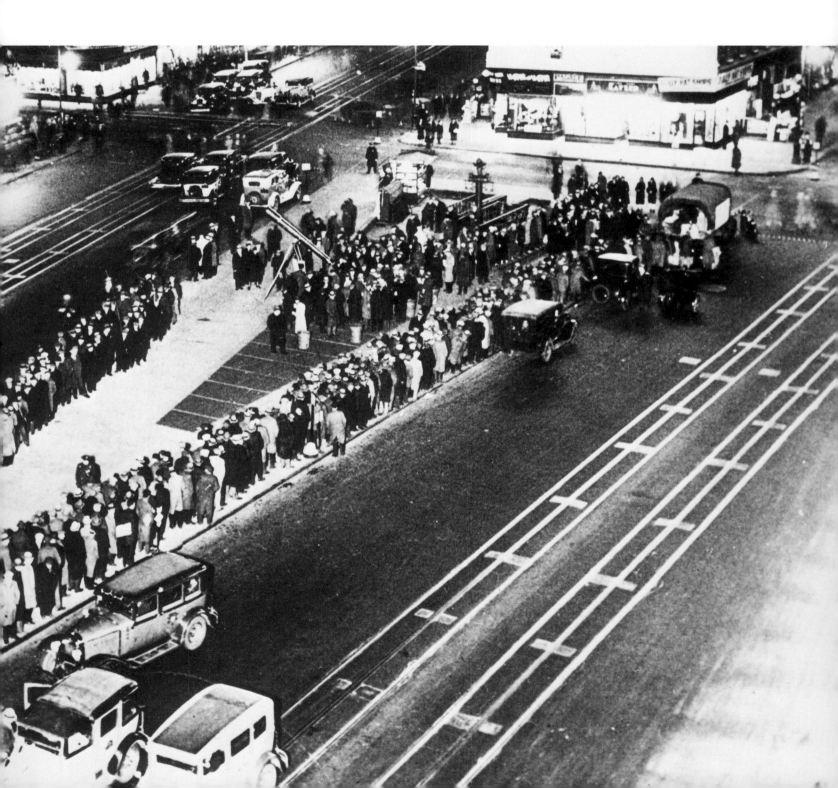

The jobless swamped the employment agencies during the decade. Often people paid employment agencies their last few dollars to find them work which lasted only two or three days.

President Hoover, Can You Spare a Dime?

At first it seemed that President Herbert Hoover did not believe there was a serious Depression. On March 7, 1930, he told Americans that the Depression would be over in another 60 days. Hoover believed that American businesses would take care of themselves. He promised that in time, without help from the government, things would return to normal.

Hoover did have a couple of interesting ideas on how to help hungry Americans. In 1931 he told a reporter, "What this country needs is a good big laugh. . . . If someone could get off a good joke every ten days, I think our troubles would be over." And to the famous singer Rudee Vallee, Hoover promised, "If you can sing a song that will make people forget their troubles and the depression, I'll give you a medal."

But the song heard most during the Hoover years was, "Brother, Can You Spare a Dime?" Jack rabbits, caught on the western plains for food, were nicknamed Hoover hogs. Camptowns of poor people, where hundreds of tiny shelters were made of tin, cardboard, and wood scraps, became known as Hoovervilles. And old newspapers used by the homeless on cold nights, were called Hoover blankets.

"What this country needs is a good big laugh . . ." President Hoover said.

In time, Hoover did take some action to help American businesses. But in the case of the Smoot-Hawley Tariff Act, the action hurt more than it helped. In 1930 Hoover signed the bill that would raise tariffs, or taxes, on incoming goods to the United States. Hoover believed this would stop the import of European goods. He thought that American businesses would then have a bigger share of the market. But many of these European countries were also in depressions. These countries resented the tariff act. They reacted against the United States by raising their tariffs on American goods.

The American farmer was hurt most by the bill. No longer did Europe buy America's plentiful crops. And in the Depression years, farmers grew more food and raised more animals than people could buy. One farmer found it would cost him $1.10 to ship each of his sheep to market. But once there, the sheep would only bring him $1.00 each. ⇨

During the depression soup kitchens fed thousands of Americans.

It was useless to sell the sheep, and he had no money to feed them. So he cut their throats and let the meat rot while Americans went hungry.

Hoover finally took a positive step in 1932. He started the Reconstruction Finance Corporation (RFC). This government agency loaned money to banks and big businesses that were about to fail. But for most Americans, the creation of the RFC was too little, too late. ■

Wood and tar paper shacks set up by the unemployed along New York's Riverside Drive in 1932. Small communities such as these were called "Hoovervilles" in "honor" of President Herbert Hoover.

Bullets for Bread

In March 1931 the famous car-maker, Henry Ford, said, "The average man won't really do a day's work unless he is caught and cannot get out of it. There is plenty of work to do if people would do it."

One year later, the average man showed Mr. Ford how badly he wanted work. Three thousand jobless men marched, unarmed, to Ford's car plant in Dearborn, Michigan. They only wanted jobs. But they were met by police and firemen. The firemen sprayed the men with icy water, scattering them in all directions. Police shot tear gas into the crowd, and then opened fire with guns. In the end, four marchers lay dead. Many more were hurt.

The funeral for the dead workers was held in Detroit two days later. Thousands marched in the streets, hardly believing what had happened. They carried red signs, signaling danger. The signs read, "Ford gave bullets for bread."

Veterans Protest
The Army Against the Army

Soldiers used tear gas to break up the Bonus Army veterans protest in Washington, D.C. in July, 1932.

By 1932 the jobless were protesting. Farmers were striking and refusing to send any food to market. And a group of war veterans had gone to Washington, D.C. to ask for help. This last group called itself the Bonus Expeditionary Force or the Bonus Army.

In 1924 Congress had passed a bill. This bill promised a cash bonus to soldiers who fought in the Great War. It said that the bonus was to be paid in 1945. But in 1932 a new bill asked that the veterans be paid immediately.

Many veterans were in favor of this new bill. After all, with the Depression on, they weren't sure they'd live to see that 1945 bonus. So 20,000 of these men went to Washington, D.C. to show how they felt. They had risked their lives to help America in 1917. Now they wanted to be repaid when they needed help the most.

When they got to Washington, the men camped where they could. Many built shelters of wood and paper near the Anacostia River. The camps were clean and orderly, as if the men were still serving in the army. Some men stayed in empty government buildings in Washington.

The House of Representatives passed the bonus bill. But the Senate did not. The veterans felt as if President Hoover and the leaders of Washington had slapped them in the face. On July 28, the Washington police were ordered to clear the Bonus Army out of the government buildings. Then one of the saddest events of the Great Depression occurred.

The Bonus Army refused to go. Fights broke out. The police shot and killed two men. Fearing more trouble, President Hoover called on the United States army. General Douglas MacArthur ordered the veterans to be out of Washington in one hour. At the end of the hour he let his troops loose. They charged, bayonets first, through the Bonus Army's town on the Anacostia River. They threw tear gas, killing an eleven-month-old baby. By the evening of July 29, the Bonus Army had scattered. Their poor cardboard shacks were set on fire.

Both President Hoover and General MacArthur believed they had done what was necessary. But most Americans could only hang their heads in shame. In November, Americans elected a new president. They hoped Franklin Delano Roosevelt would lead them out of the dark hole called the Great Depression. ■

President Roosevelt Promises A "New Deal"

The day: March 4. The year: 1933. The place: Washington, D.C. The event: inauguration day. Franklin D. Roosevelt officially steps into the office of president of the United States.

Crowds wait eagerly for the new president's speech. The nation is tired of the depression, hungry for food, and desperate for hope.

Roosevelt takes the oath of office. This new president wears braces on his legs. But on this day, even in the cold Washington wind, he looks tall and strong. His voice carries across the crowd.

"The only thing we have to fear is fear itself. . . . " he tells the people. "This nation asks for action, and action now. We must act and act quickly . . .

"The people of the United States have not failed. . . .They have asked for discipline and direction under leadership. They have made me an instrument of their wishes. In the spirit of the gift, I take it."

The people love the speech. President Hoover had not been able to help Americans in the Depression years. This new president promises action.

And from March 9 to June 16, 1933, FDR generated plenty of action. Those now famous "hundred days" will be remembered for decades to come.

The Hundred Days

The inauguration ball was held the evening of March 4 without the president. FDR went straight to his office, ready to work. The banking problem had to be tackled. Each day more and more American banks were failing. FDR began by making Monday, March 6, a "banking holiday." All banks across the country would be closed until the U.S. Treasury Department could examine their books. Those that were found to be in good financial condition would be allowed to reopen.

While FDR worked, Americans tried to learn to get along without money. In Salt Lake City, people traded toothpaste and stockings for rides on the city buses. A good pair of tickets to a boxing match in New York City could be traded for a pair of shoes. One person said that if the banks had closed for good, Americans would have learned to do without money altogether.

> "The only thing we have to fear, is fear itself."

When banks finally reopened, the Treasury Department looked closely at their finances. Americans were pleased that the government was doing something—anything. Some trust in government returned.

Franklin Roosevelt (center) is sworn in as the nation's 32d president in 1933.

President Roosevelt signs into law one of the many bills Congress enacted during his first term.

The familiar NRA member sign could be found in thousands of businesses during the decade.

Soon more and more people began to leave their money in banks once again.

The banking holiday was just the beginning of what Roosevelt called the New Deal for America. The New Deal was made up of a number of programs which people called "alphabet soup." It began with the Agricultural Adjustment Administration, or the AAA.

The AAA was supposed to help farmers. It stopped banks from taking land from farmers who could not pay their bills. And it tried to drive up farm prices by getting rid of surplus farm goods. To drive up the price of pork, for example, more than six million baby pigs were killed. And farmers were paid **not** to grow certain kinds of crops. Many people felt it was un-American to pay people to stop working. But for a while, the suffering of some farmers eased somewhat.

More Popular Programs

FDR also created the Civilian Conservation Corps. The CCC put young men from the ages of 18 to

25 to work. The young men planted trees for one dollar a day plus room and board. Some people argued that the young men were treated like slaves. But many of the 25,000 boys in the CCC were simply glad to be off the streets.

The Federal Emergency Relief Administration (FERA) gave a half billion dollars to state programs. The money was used to get America's jobless back to work. The Federal Deposit Insurance Corporation (FDIC) insured bank deposits of up to $5,000.

One of the most popular programs was the National Recovery Administration (NRA). Under the NRA, each industry had to follow certain rules. The rules had to do with

what workers were paid, how many hours they worked, and competition among businesses. Everyone soon recognized the signs with the NRA symbol, a blue eagle with the words, "We do our part." These signs could be found in businesses all over America. Hollywood bathing beauties were even seen with a drawing of the NRA symbol on their bare backs.

In April of 1932, FDR told Congress of his plan for the Tennessee Valley Authority (TVA). One of the poorest pockets of the country was around the Tennessee River. Once green and forested, the land was bare of trees. Poor farming practices had caused much of the good farmland to blow away. And

yearly floods had washed away even more soil.

The TVA, a federal agency, would take back this land and make it work. Dams would be built to stop flooding. Electricity from the dams would be sold, bringing energy and jobs. Farmers would be taught how to plant and grow crops that would not hurt the land.

Many people in government shook their heads at the idea of the TVA. They thought Roosevelt's government was starting to take control in too many ways. Now it was getting into the business of producing and selling power!

But the TVA, along with the other alphabet soup programs, was passed by Congress anyway. In June, the first hundred days of Roosevelt's term were over. He left the White House for a much needed rest. And the American people had time to catch their breath. ∎

FDR (waving, in car) visits members of a Civilian Conservation Corps to give them some personal encouragement.

A Close Call for FDR

Franklin D. Roosevelt almost didn't live to take office.

On February 16, 1933, FDR gave a speech in Miami, Florida. As he got into his car, he heard what sounded to him like firecrackers. Bullets, meant for him, hit five others. Chicago's Mayor Anton Cermak was killed.

The killer, caught immediately, was Guiseppe Zangara. Said Zangara that day, "I hate all presidents, no matter from what country they come and I hate all officials and everybody who is rich . . . I'd kill every president, I'd kill them all."

Manufacturing alcohol became legal once again when Prohibition was repealed in 1933.

Prohibition Ends

Americans Drink Up—Legally

The story goes like this. President Franklin D. Roosevelt has just started his first term as president. On the evening of March 12, 1933, he's in the White House enjoying his dinner. He leans back in his chair and says thoughtfully, "I think this would be a good time for a beer." With those words, Prohibition was on its way out.

The Eighteenth Amendment, also called Prohibition, had been added to the Constitution in 1919. It had prohibited the manufacture and sale of alcoholic drinks throughout the United States.

For years, everyone had known that Prohibition did not work. Gangsters, like Al Capone, made big

---

Move over, Al Capone. Here comes Uncle Sam!

---

money as bootleggers. They made and sold illegal alcohol by the gallon. Many Americans went to illegal bars called "speakeasies" to drink. So

what had been gained? Crime was growing and Americans were still drinking.

It didn't take Congress long to act on FDR's suggestion. A bill was quickly passed. Now it was legal for Americans to sell drinks with an alcohol content of 3.7% or less.

On April 7, 1933, Americans had their first legal taste of "near beer" and light wines in nearly fourteen years. On that day alone, the federal government collected between $7 and $10 million in taxes from beer sales. Move over, Al Capone. Here comes Uncle Sam! ■

35

Seven of the Scottsboro boys, shown here, with one of their attorneys, Samuel Leibowitz (second from left).

The Scottsboro Court Case

A Nightmare That Doesn't End

The date was April 6, 1931. The people of Scottsboro, Alabama, were having a grand time. Music was playing and drinks were being sold in the streets.

What was the occasion? Thousands had come out to see the Scottsboro boys—nine Negroes, all but one in his teens. Tied together, they were led from the jail to the courthouse. The crowd pressed toward them. "You niggers gonna die," they yelled. "You niggers gonna die."

The case of the Scottsboro boys lasted seven years. This is their story.

During the worst of the Depression years, there were thousands of jobless people. Many of them hopped the freight trains and rode from town to town, looking for work. On March 25, 1931, a group of Negroes and a group of whites tried to ride in the same freight car. A fight broke out and the whites were kicked off the train. The fight was reported in

Stevenson, Alabama. The train was searched two stops later. Ten male youths—nine black and one white— were taken from the train. Two white women, both dressed like men in overalls, were also found.

While the blacks were being questioned, the white women stood by quietly. Then after a few minutes, one of the women called to a deputy. She said that she and her friend had been raped by the nine blacks. It took just minutes for the word to spread. The nine blacks were charged with rape and taken to jail in Scottsboro.

The people of Scottsboro crowded around the jail that night, wanting to lynch the nine young men. But the city officials talked them out of it. Justice, they said, would be done in the trial.

The court appointed a lawyer to defend the Scottsboro boys. The laywer had a well-known drinking problem. And he had no time to talk to the boys before the trial.

Evidence against the Scottsboro boys was slim. Victoria Price, one of the two women, took the stand. She said she had been raped by all nine blacks. So had her friend, Ruby Bates. They said that they had been left beaten and bloody.

But the doctor who had examined both women had a different story. He said there was no evidence of rape. As far as he could tell, neither woman had been bruised or harmed in any way. Much later, the doctor told a judge outside of court, "I looked at both women and told them they were lying, that they knew they had not been raped. They just laughed at me."

Eight of the boys were found guilty and sentenced to death. The case of the youngest, a thirteen year old, was declared a mistrial.

Supreme Court Appeal

The International Labor Defense, a part of the Communist party, came to the aid of the Scottsboro boys. Lawyer Sam Leibowitz took the case all the way to the United States Supreme Court. In November 1932 the Court ruled for the Scottsboro boys. The ruling said they had been denied the right to a fair trial because of their first lawyer's poor skills. So the case was tried again—this time in Decatur, Alabama.

"... she might be a fallen woman, but by God she is a white woman."

Leibowitz turned up more evidence in favor of the Scottsboro boys. On the stand, Victoria Price changed her story many times. She and Bates were both found to be prostitutes. Ruby Bates said she had lied. She admitted that neither she nor Price had been raped. But the Scottsboro boys were once again found guilty and sentenced to death. Said one Alabama citizen of Victoria Price, "... (she) might be a fallen woman, but by God she is a white woman."

Leibowitz took the case back to the Supreme Court. How could the trial be fair, he argued, when no blacks were allowed on any juries in Alabama? On April 1, 1935, the Court agreed. And once again, in 1937, the case went to trial.

The same evidence came to light. By now many people across America were calling for the Scottsboro boys to be freed. Yet, four of the boys were found guilty: Clarence Norris was sentenced to death (later commuted to life in prison). Andy Wright got 99 years. And Charley Weems and Haywood Patterson each got 75 years. Charges were dropped against Willie Robertson, Olen Montgomery, Eugene Williams, and Roy Wright. All had already spent seven years in jail.

Many people have called on Alabama's governor to pardon the Scottsboro boys. Others say that justice has been done. But for four of the Scottsboro boys, the nightmare goes on. ■

Protesters march outside the White House demanding justice for the Scottsboro boys.

Lindbergh Baby Kidnapped

The Crime of the Decade

Who can forget the terrible facts of the crime? The handsome American hero, his loving wife, and their first child, a healthy, curly-haired boy, just twenty months old. An open window, a noise in the night, a note asking for money. And later—the child's hand seemingly reaching out from a shallow grave. The kidnapping of Charles and Anne Lindbergh's baby will be remembered as the crime of the decade.

The Lindberghs were famous long before the kidnapping. Charles Lindbergh became America's hero in 1927 when he flew his airplane from New York to Paris. He was the first man to fly solo across the Atlantic Ocean, and he did it in 33½ hours. Later, he and his wife Anne explored the sky together, flying new routes for America's growing airplane industry. Newspaper reporters followed the Lindberghs everywhere. Any story about the famous Charles and Anne sold papers. The young couple began to think they would never be left alone.

Their first child was born in June of 1930. It was then that the Lindberghs decided it was time to find some peace. During the week, they stayed with Anne's parents in Englewood, New Jersey. But on weekends, the Lindberghs went into hiding. Their hiding place, also in New Jersey, was the Hopewell House. It was a comfortable home in the country, circled by land and forests. There, with three servants, they lived a quiet family life. It was a peace that did not last long.

A Sound in the Night

It had been a long winter. Anne Lindbergh and baby Charles both had colds. On Sunday, February 28, 1932, they decided to stay at the Hopewell House instead of going to Englewood for the week. On Monday, as usual, Charles Lindbergh went to work in New York. But on Tuesday, he drove back to Hopewell to be with his family.

> ## "Anne, they have stolen our child."

When he arrived at 8:30 P.M., his son had already been asleep for an hour. He had been tucked in by the family nurse. Charles sat up and talked with Anne and did not look in on the boy. A little after nine, Charles thought he heard the sound of wood breaking. But he was tired from his long drive and he didn't investigate the noise.

At ten o'clock that night, the Lindbergh's nurse went into the baby's room. An open window had made the room cold. The nurse turned on a heater and tried to warm her hands before picking up the baby. But to her shock, there was no baby to pick up.

The nurse first ran to Anne, then to Charles. "Do you have the baby?" she asked with worry. Charles and Anne ran to their son's room. They saw a white envelope in the open window.

Charles Lindbergh knew what had happened. "Anne, they have stolen our child," he said.

The police came right away. The note in the envelope asked for $50,000. It said the Lindberghs would be contacted later with directions on how to get the money to the kidnapper. Only then would the couple get their child back. The note was signed with two circles overlapping each other.

The police also found a wooden ladder in the woods outside the Lindberghs' home. One step of the ladder was broken.

It wasn't long before the newspapers got wind of the

Police search the home and garage of Bruno Hauptmann, who was later arrested for the murder of Charles Lindbergh's son.

Lindbergh case. And once again, Charles and Anne were front page news. "Lindy's Baby Kidnapped!" screamed the headlines on March 2, 1932.

Letters offering help and words of comfort began pouring into the Lindberghs' home. Then New York governor, Franklin D. Roosevelt, said the state police could help in the case. Even Al Capone, the famous Chicago gangster, wanted to give $10,000 to help find the baby. A retired school teacher named Dr. John Condon put a letter in the Bronx Home News saying he would give an extra $1,000 for return of the baby. Two days later Condon got a letter telling him to act as a go-between. When Condon told the Lindberghs the letter was signed with two overlapping circles, the Lindberghs decided to use his offer of help.

Condon met with the kidnapper a few times. The kidnapper called himself "John." "John" had a German accent. It seemed that these meetings were to test whether Condon and the Lindberghs could be trusted.

Finally, on March 31, "John"

sent Condon a note. He wanted the money ready on April 2. Lindbergh drove Condon to St. Raymond's Cemetery, where Condon and "John" were supposed to meet. Condon walked in front of the cemetery a few times, but saw no one. Then a voice called out "Hey, Doctor!" just as Condon was about to leave. Charles Lindbergh said he would never forget the sound of that voice.

The money was given to "John" in exchange for a note telling where the baby could be found. The Lindbergh baby was on a boat, it said, and gave directions on where to find him. Lindbergh and Condon were full of hope as they drove away from the cemetery that night.

Tragedy in the Woods

The boat, however, was not where the note said it would be. Weeks went by with no further word from the kidnapper. On May 12, 1932, Lindbergh was at sea following another lead on his son's whereabouts when bad news came. A truck driver had stopped near the

Lindberghs' home. At the edge of the woods, the driver had pushed aside some dirt with his foot. The hand of a small child appeared. It was the body of baby Charles. The child had been hit in the head and killed the same night he had been kidnapped.

The Lindberghs buried their young son and tried to forget. They went on to make more record-breaking flights together. And they had their second son, Jon. Charles bought a large police dog to guard Jon. He protected his son in every possible way.

Then in September 1934, news came that an arrest had been made in the Lindbergh kidnapping case. And for the Lindberghs, the awful past once again came alive.

While the Lindberghs had been trying to forget, the police were looking for the murderer. The money given to the kidnapper had been partly made up of special gold notes. Stores and banks were asked to take down the license number of any person using such notes. Finally a New York City bank reported a person with the car license of ⇨

4U–13–41. The car belonged to Bruno Richard Hauptmann, a German-American carpenter living in the Bronx. The police found $13,000 of the kidnap money in the Hauptmann garage. The Department of Agriculture was able to trace the wooden ladder to Hauptmann. Later, John Condon identified Hauptmann as "John." And Charles Lindbergh identified Hauptmann's voice as the one he heard cry, "Hey, Doctor," that night in the cemetery.

The trial was one of the biggest public events of the decade. Thousands of people gathered outside the New Jersey courthouse. They wanted to see the famous Lindberghs, and the now famous Hauptmann and his wife. During the trial, people sold supposed locks of the Lindbergh baby's hair for $5.

Hauptmann had been charged not with kidnapping, but with murder. Hauptmann's lawyer made a good case for his client. Even if Hauptmann had been involved in the kidnapping, others must have been in on it, too. How, he asked, could a baby be taken from the Lindberghs' home so quietly? Wasn't it possible that a servant had handed the baby over to the kidnapper? Wasn't it possible that Dr. Condon had also been a part of the crime? What evidence was there, beyond a doubt, that Hauptmann had killed the child? None. But the jury did not agree. In March of 1935, Bruno Richard Hauptmann was convicted of murder and was sentenced to death. He was executed in April 1936.

On December 22, 1935, the Lindberghs moved to England. More kidnapping threats, daily newspaper stories, and lack of privacy had driven them away.

At the end of the decade they returned to the United States. The couple said they hoped that all Americans could leave the crime behind them, just as they had tried to. But it's unlikely that Americans will ever forget the kidnapping and murder of baby Charles. ∎

Bruno Hauptmann (second from right) at his trial in 1935.

"Scarface" Al Capone (center) smiles with his lawyers at his trial for income tax evasion. After the trial, Al wasn't smiling.

Scarface Al's Luck Runs Out

"I've been made an issue, I guess, and I'm not complaining. But why don't they go after all these bankers who took the savings of thousands of poor people and lost them in the bank failures? How about that?

Isn't it lots worse to take the last few dollars some family has saved . . . than to sell a little beer?"

—Alphonse "Scarface" Capone

Yeah. Capone sold a little beer. They say his business was worth about $100 million a year. And true, he didn't hurt poor people, except to sell them liquor. He did figure in hundreds of bloody gang murders, though. And many Americans were glad to see Al put behind bars in 1931. The charge? He hadn't paid his taxes.

Al Capone grew up in the tough streets of Brooklyn, New York.

There he learned to handle guns, knives, and use his fists. One lesson showed on his face: a deep scar, from left ear to mouth, put there by an enemy's razor.

Capone was 23 years old and working as a dishwasher when a friend helped him get a new job. The job was in Chicago. Capone became the right-hand man of Johnny Torrio, a bootlegger. Together they supplied the gangs of Chicago with barrels and barrels of illegal beer and liquor. Torrio decided to retire after recovering from a few gunshot wounds. Before he left for Italy, he shook Capone's hand. "It's all yours, Al," he said. At that time, they were making $60 million a year.

What followed is history. Capone became one of the most powerful men in Chicago. He controlled the mayor, the city council, and many of the police.

(Once, Capone's gang members clubbed uncooperative city council members on the head during a council meeting.)

Rival gangs had to do business Al's way—or else. Capone ordered the St. Valentine's Day massacre, in which seven Chicago hoodlums were gunned down. In another case, gang leader Dion O'Banion got six bullets from Capone's gunmen. (Good-hearted Capone sent $8,000 worth of flowers to O'Banion's funeral, too.) Many lawmen and lawbreakers tried to take Al down. But the bullets always missed.

Then in 1931, Al's luck ran out. He was arrested for not paying his taxes. On October 25, 1931, he was sentenced to 11 years in prison. Said Al, "Well, I'm on my way to do 11 years. I've got to do it and that's all. I'm not sore at anybody. Some people are lucky. I wasn't." ∎

A Decade of Dangerous Men (and Women)

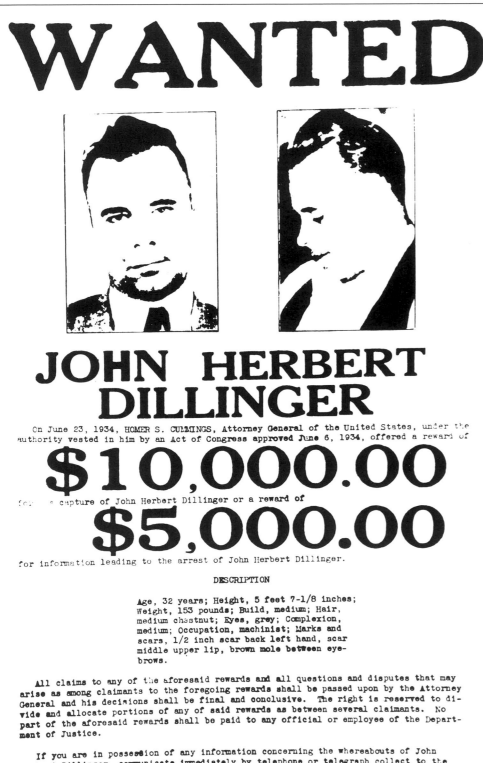

Jobs were hard to come by during the Depression. Many people grew desperate. But it's hard to excuse the outlaws who made a living by robbing and killing. Stories about these gun-carrying men and women filled the newspapers during the decade. It was exciting reading, until you became an unlucky victim of this heartless bunch. Below is a rundown of some of the most famous criminals of the 1930s.

The Barker Gang: Ma Barker and her four boys, Herman, Lloyd, Arthur or "Doc," and Fred, were called the Barker Gang. The family, living penniless in tar paper shacks, turned to crime during the 1920s. Once they got going, they robbed banks and killed without mercy. Some said Ma Barker, called "Bloody Mama" by the newspapers, was the brains of the family. She planned the jobs right down to the getaway route. By 1935, Ma and Freddie were all that was left of the gang. The others had been killed or were in jail. A four hour gun battle finally put an end to the rest of the Barker gang.

Bank robber John Dillinger was on the FBI's Ten Most Wanted List in the 1930s.

Pretty Boy Floyd: As a boy, Charles Arthur Floyd was often seen combing his greasy, slick-backed hair. From that came the name "Pretty Boy." But Floyd's life was anything but pretty.

He was raised in Oklahoma, the son of sharecroppers. In 1924 he married a 16 year old. With his first child on the way, he decided that the only way to make a living was to rob banks. And though he killed many people who crossed his path, Floyd never forgot to do something nice. In small towns, he threw money from the window of his getaway car into the streets. He also tore up home mortgages while he was in the bank. Back home in Oklahoma, Pretty Boy Floyd was a hero.

In October 1934 eight FBI bullets ended the hometown hero's life.

Bonnie and Clyde: This pair was small-time compared to the Barkers and Floyd. Bonnie Parker and Clyde Barrow robbed gas stations, stores, and a few small banks. They also killed 13 people.

This entertaining couple liked to send their own photos to the newspapers. Bonnie, who was a poet when she wasn't robbing people, sent in her writings. Her last, "The Ballad of Bonnie and Clyde," ended like this:

Some day they will go down together,
And they will bury them side by side,
To a few it means grief,
To the law it's relief,
But it's death to Bonnie and Clyde.

In May 1934, a Texas lawman trapped the couple. Forty bullets later the "Ballad of Bonnie and Clyde" became a true story.

John Dillinger, with a "friend" in each hand. When the FBI caught up with him in 1934, his "friends" were of no help.

Baby Face Nelson: Even the toughest of gangsters thought Baby Face Nelson was crazy. He lost his job as one of Al Capone's thugs when he killed people who were only supposed to be roughed up. Later, he became a member of the Dillinger gang. After Dillinger's death, Nelson's dream of a lifetime came true. He became the FBI's Public Enemy Number One. He lost his standing in November 1934 when he was shot and killed by the FBI.

John Dillinger: Dillinger was the most famous outlaw of the 1930s. After robbing a store when he was 21, he spent nine years in prison. There he learned the tricks of the trade he would later practice so well.

Dillinger got out of prison in May 1933. Immediately, he went on a bank-robbing spree, killing dozens of people along the way. In the next year he took in well over $100,000 from banks in Indiana, Wisconsin, Pennsylvania, and Illinois. Twice he escaped from jail. The most daring of these escapes took place in March 1934. First he locked 33 jailers and inmates into cells of the Lake County jail. Next he took two machine guns and climbed the prison walls. Dillinger then drove past 50 guards in a sheriff's car. Later he told his sister, "Pulling that off was worth ten years of my life. Ha, Ha."

But Dillinger was not laughing when the FBI caught up with him outside a Chicago theater in July 1934. The next day, newspapers across the country carried pictures of the criminal's bullet-filled body. Said Dillinger's father, "I want people to know that I tried to bring him up right and he's always been a good-hearted boy." ∎

43

Some dust storms moved as fast as 90 miles per hour across the Great Plains.

America's Great Plains

The Tragedy of the Dust Bowl

They'd seen storms before, and some of them were pretty bad. Farmers couldn't help but see bad storms on the Great Plains. Such things as summer heat above 100 degrees, twisters, snowbanks 20 feet high are all part of life there. They make farmers tough. But the people of the Great Plains had never seen anything quite like the storm they had in 1934.

On May 9, a cloud of brown dust swelled up from the plains of Montana and Wyoming. It blew forcefully toward North and South Dakota. The cloud thickened as it moved east. By the time it reached Chicago, dirt was falling from the sky like snow. On May 11, the cloud reached the Atlantic Ocean. Midwestern and Eastern Americans had just seen one of the worst dust storms in history. Suddenly, they

knew what life was like in the Dust Bowl.

The Dust Bowl is an area of the Great Plains. It covers parts of Kansas, Colorado, New Mexico, Oklahoma, and Texas. From 1933 to 1939, dust storms and dry weather turned this farmland into a bleak desert wasteland. How did it happen?

The early 1930s was a period of drought. In those years, little or no rain fell on the southern Great Plains. When the drought combined with high heat, sometimes above 110 degrees, the earth dried and cracked. Normally, the hardy grass of the Great Plains would have held this dry earth in place. But when the winds came in 1934, the grasslands were gone. During and after the Great War, farmers had gradually plowed away the grasslands. Winter wheat was planted, but the wheat didn't hold the soil. So when the windstorms of the 1930s hit, the land could simply blow away.

And blow away it did. The Soil Conservation Corps kept track of the storms where visibility was less than one mile. In 1933 there were 14 such storms. In 1935 there were 40.

And in 1938 a record 61 storms hit. More than 850 million tons of earth were lost to the winds.

The storms were damaging and fierce. Imagine a wall of dust, five miles high as it raced over the plains at speeds of up to 60 miles per hour. Cars stopped. People ran for cover. The storm might last for minutes or hours. When it was over, everyone around coughed and wiped dust from their eyes.

One seven-year-old boy was not so lucky. He wandered away in a storm. Later he was found dead in a high drift of dust. Unprotected animals had the same fate. Dead cattle, horses, birds, and rabbits were found scattered across the land. All were choked by the storms.

Money from FDR, But No Rain

By 1934 the Dust Bowl was worse than ever. President Roosevelt decided that something had to be done. He paid no attention to well-meaning Americans who wanted to cover the Dust Bowl with cement. Millions of federal dollars were sent to the Dust Bowl states. The money was used to feed

starving cattle and to plow ridges in the land to keep it from blowing away. The CCC replanted 10,000,000 acres of Dust Bowl farmland with forests. Lines of trees called windbreaks were set out to protect planted fields from the winds. Farmers were taught which crops to grow and how to plant them.

Still, the storms kept coming. More and more land kept blowing away. It seemed that all the money in the world couldn't stop it. "You gave us beer," the people told Roosevelt. "Now give us rain." It was the one thing that he could not do. ■

> "You gave us beer," the people told Roosevelt. "Now give us rain."

Some property was almost completely swallowed up by the dust storms.

A family left homeless by the dust storms heads west in June 1938.

Their Lives
with the

Now it wasn't just hard, it was *impossible* to make a living. The Dust Bowl farmers faced ruined land, dead livestock, and barns buried in dust. So, more than 60% of the Dust Bowl population packed up and moved on to greener pastures in the 1930s. Or so they thought.

They set out by the hundreds and thousands along the western roads, looking for work. But these were the Depression years, so there was little work to find. Western states did not want the Dust Bowlers, whom they called "Okies." These states already had enough homeless, enough jobless, enough mouths to feed. Road signs told the Okies to go home. But home was

The face of this Oklahoma woman tells the sad story of the Dust Bowl families.

Some Things Are Still Funny

Despite all their hardships and suffering, many Dust Bowlers maintained a sense of humor during their troubles. The following story illustrates the point.

A man driving a car saw a ten gallon cowboy hat resting on a high pile of dust. He stopped and lifted up the hat. Under it was the head of a farmer, alive and well.

"Can I help you?" the man asked the farmer. "I've got my car here. I can give you a ride into town."

"No thanks," said the farmer, "I can make it on my own. I'm on a horse."

Were "Gone Wind"

buried under a pile of dust now. There was no turning back.

Many of the Dust Bowlers have ended up in California. There, they travel from farm to farm picking fruit and vegetables. Pay is low. For a long day of picking grapes a worker might earn $1.25. The farm owner keeps 25 cents of this pay for rent. In return, the worker gets a floorless wooden shack to sleep in. There is no running water, no blanket. Families of eight can be found sleeping in these tiny shelters. But few argue with the owners about the pay or the conditions. For every man who will not work, there are ten to take his place. This seems to be the story of the 1930s. ■

End O' My Line

It isn't hard to find out more about Dust Bowlers. Their lives are the subjects of books, pictures, and songs. John Steinbeck's book *The Grapes of Wrath* paints a picture of their troubles with powerful and sad words. The photographs of Dorothea Lange show the hungry faces of women and children. And Woody Guthrie sings of their sorrows in his songs. This verse from Guthrie's song, *End O' My Line*, gives other Americans an idea of what the Great Plains farmers are feeling:

Long about Nineteen thirty-one
My field burnt up in the
* boiling sun.*
Long about Nineteen thirty-two,
Dust did rise and the dust it
* blew.*
End o' my line, end o' my line,
I reckon I come to the end o'
* my line.*

Two Dust Bowl refugees who weren't lucky enough to take the advice of the billboard sign.

Many Dust Bowl families moved to California. There they picked fruits and vegetables for one dollar a day.

President Roosevelt encouraged the nation many times during the decade with his "fireside chats" over the radio.

The New Deal Runs Into Trouble

Not all of Franklin Roosevelt's time as president has been as successful as his first 100 days. In 1935 the Supreme Court struck down two of Roosevelt's New Deal programs. The Agricultural Adjustment Administration (AAA) and the National Recovery Administration (NRA) were both found unconstitutional. In both cases, the Court said the federal government had overstepped its powers.

Roosevelt was angry. How could he get the country out of the Depression if his powers to act were so limited? Roosevelt believed the Supreme Court was stuck in old ways. After all, it was made up of nine "old men." The youngest man on the court was 64 and the oldest was in his 80s.

In 1936 Roosevelt was elected to his second term. He beat the Republican, Alf Landon, by 11 million votes. To Roosevelt, his landslide victory meant the American people were very much in favor of his programs. Only some "old men" in Washington were against him. So FDR decided it was time to change the Supreme Court.

In 1937 he asked Congress to pass a new law. Under the law, a Supreme Court justice would be expected to retire at the age of 70. If he did not, a younger judge would be put on the Court to help him. And the new law also said that the Supreme Court could be made up of 15 justices.

Roosevelt told Congress that this new law would be a great help to the Court. It would mean a lighter workload. More cases could be heard. But Congress knew what FDR's real purpose was. Roosevelt was trying to "pack the Court" with justices who saw things his way. Even many of Roosevelt's strong supporters were disappointed by this move. On July 22, 1937, the bill died in the Senate. Roosevelt had lost an important battle.

The Depression Goes On

FDR continued to try to strengthen the country with his New Deal programs. In 1935 Congress passed the Social Security Act. This program set up old-age and unemployment insurance for 26 million Americans. Another new law strengthened unions. And another one heavily taxed the fortunes the rich pass on through inheritance.

The Works Progress Administration (WPA) also put many people to work. Artists hired by the WPA painted scenes of the times on city buildings. In some ways, they brought beauty and hope to the worst years of the Depression.

Yet, the Depression was not cured by the New Deal. In 1937 the stock market crashed again. In 1938 ten million people were still out of work. Roosevelt asked Congress for more than a half billion dollars to spend on work programs. He got it. But no one was sure if even this much money would bring the country out of its misery.

By the end of the decade, however, the American economy was showing signs of new life. Many factories were once again humming. People were working. Goods were being produced. But they were not the goods of peace time. They were guns, battleships, and tanks.

Countries across the ocean had gone to war once again. And once again America had vowed to stay out of it. But whether or not she did, America's industries were making sure the country was ready for anything. ■

World's Tallest Building Goes Up

The Depression years were not without some high points. The highest was the top of the Empire State building—1,472 feet above the street!

The ground breaking for the world's tallest building took place on March 17, 1930. After that it took a little more than a year to finish the last of the 102 stories. On May 1, 1931, opening ceremonies were led by President Herbert Hoover and New York governor, Al Smith.

At the beginning of the Depression, however, few businesses had enough money to move into the $40 million building. For many years, the building stayed nearly empty, towering grandly over the breadlines below.

But whether it's filled with people or not, New Yorkers love the Empire State building. It is truly an amazing piece of work. More than 400 tons of steel and 6,400 windows went into its construction. It even has a dock for high-flying dirigibles or "blimps."

People planning a trip to New York shouldn't miss it. The building is located on 34th Street and Fifth Avenue. Visitors can enjoy taking a trip up to the 86th floor observation deck. Or they can ride the elevators to the very top—the 102d floor, 1,250 feet above the street. There, visitors often find themselves above the rain clouds. In a storm, they have to watch out for lightning, which often hits the building. And they have to hang on when the mighty Empire moves back and forth with the winds. But even on a clear, calm day, a trip to the top is truly an unforgettable experience. ∎

Mighty Boulder Dam

The Wonder of the West

The Empire State Building may be the building wonder of the East Coast. But far to the West, another great project was completed in this decade. It was Boulder Dam, one of the highest dams in the world.

The Boulder Dam was built to tame the Colorado River. For years, the river had devastated farms and ranches in Arizona. Floods often wiped out a whole year's growing season. Then at dry times, crops died from lack of water.

The Boulder Dam solves all that. Its great cement walls store huge amounts of Colorado River water in a reservoir called Lake Mead. During dry times, this reserved water is sent to thirsty lands. During times of flood, the reservoir holds back the dangerous waters. And the dam also uses the water to make electricity. Sale of this energy source helps to hold down the cost of running the dam.

The Boulder Dam is quite a sight. Finished in 1936, it is 725 feet high—more than 44 stories. It runs 2,244 feet in length. The concrete that went into it could pave a road more than 2,000 miles long.

The dam's reservoir is like a blue jewel in the middle of the desert. Lake Mead is one of the world's largest man-made lakes. It is 115 miles long and almost 600 feet deep. And the people of the dry Southwest love Lake Mead for more than its practical uses of water. It is also used for boating, fishing, and swimming. In many ways, Boulder Dam has created a magnificent park. ∎

The Boulder Dam, the newest wonder of the West.

Blast–off in New Mexico

It was late December 1935. Professor Robert H. Goddard invited some American newspaper reporters to his Mescalero Ranch in New Mexico. When the reporters arrived, Goddard showed them films of his experiments with rockets. Many of those present were amazed at what they saw.

The films showed rockets, about 11 feet long and weighing between 58 to 85 pounds, sailing more than 4,000 feet into the sky! Powered by liquid fuel, the rockets did not travel in a straight line. Some observers said they looked like fish swimming up into space. A trail of black smoke marked their paths in the sky.

What Goddard had captured on film was the result of years of hard work by him and his co-workers. In 1939 Goddard had written a scientific paper outlining his ideas for making rockets. He believed that liquid fuels could be used to power rockets far into space. Someday, he wrote, rockets could possibly reach the moon.

Not many people believed in Goddard's ideas then. But he did manage to get some money for his work. On March 16, 1923, the first rocket was launched in Auburn, Massachusetts. It traveled 184 feet in 2.5 seconds. It had gone faster than 60 miles per hour!

In 1930 Goddard was forced to leave Massachusetts for New Mexico. The firechief in Auburn didn't like the idea of rockets setting the New England forests on fire! New Mexico proved a good home for his project.

On Mescalero Ranch, his rockets could fly and crash in the open country without much danger to anyone.

On December 30, 1930, Goddard tested a rocket powered by liquid oxygen and gasoline. It flew 2,000 feet high at 500 miles per hour. In March 1935 another rocket traveled 4,800 feet into the air. Amazingly, it had reached a speed of 550 miles per hour.

What does Goddard see as the future for his rockets? He would like to see them used for exploring space. Others warn that the rockets might someday be used as weapons of war. But who knows, Goddard's original idea may be correct. Someday, these rockets may just take a man to the moon. ∎

One of Dr. Robert Goddard's rockets is prepared for launching at his Mescalero Ranch in New Mexico.

New York Holds a World's Fair

New York's spectacular 1939 World's Fair. The Trylon (left) and Perisphere (right) were symbols of the fair's World of Tomorrow theme.

On April 30th, 1939, the New York World's Fair opened its doors. Called the World of Tomorrow, the glamorous fair had rather dirty beginnings. It was built on the site of the old Corona Dump garbage pit in Queens. But lots of fill dirt turned the smelly dump into lovely Flushing Meadows Park, complete with a river and man-made lake. The fairgrounds, 3 miles long and 1.5 miles wide, can hold 350,000 visitors.

At the center of the fair were the white Trylon and Perisphere buildings. The Trylon stood 700 feet high. Shaped like a triangle, this three-sided building was used as a broadcast tower during the fair. A light from its pointed top could be seen for miles around.

The Perisphere was an 18-story, round building. A small-sized city of the future was built inside it. Its name: Democracity. At night, lighted fountains sparkled around the Perisphere. At a distance, it looked as though the Perisphere building itself floated on the tips of the water.

In many ways, the World's Fair truly was a city of the future. There fairgoers saw an amazing new building material called plastic. Others were surprised and pleased with the invention of "television." Real sights and sounds actually came from this strange box. Imagine one day having one in your own living room!

The railroad exhibit took the most space at the fair. Old steam engines and high-speed trains proudly took their place in the past

and the future. Another popular exhibit was the airplane building. All kinds of planes, both big and small, hung from a ceiling. Small children stared with delight, and pretended to feel the wind from the propellers.

There was plenty more to see in the 200 buildings holding exhibits from around the world. Art, music, food, and colorful flags were everywhere. Gracing the lake were Billy Rose and his Aquabelles. This group of beauties danced, swam, and sang to the cheers of thousands.

Unfortunately the fair was a money-loser for New York state. But something of value was gained. The fair made New Yorkers feel proud and hopeful after the decade-long Depression. For that reason alone, it was worth every penny. ■

51

Babe Didrikson Stars at 1932 Olympics

What if they held an Olympics and nobody came? In 1932 that was the fear of city leaders in Los Angeles. Countries all around the world were deep in economic depressions. Would they have the money to send the world's best athletes all the way to America?

But come they did. Two thousand athletes, from 69 nations, came to strut their stuff in sunny Los Angeles that summer. The athletes from Brazil worked especially hard to get there. Since Brazil had no money, 69 Brazilian athletes and 50,000 bags of coffee were put on a ship for the United States. Along the way, the athletes stopped at various ports and sold the coffee. Sadly, they only earned enough money for 24 of the athletes to get off the ship. The rest had to sail away, in search of more coffee markets.

The games opened on July 30, 1932. More than 100,000 people watched as Vice-President Charles Curtis gave the opening speech. Then, a colorful parade showed off the many fine men and women who had come to compete. There were 500 athletes from the United States. Japan had the next largest number with 142. China, a country of 400 million people, sent only one athlete.

Every Olympic Games has its star, and Olympiad X was no different. This time it was an American— and a woman—who shone brighter than all the others. Her name was Mildred "Babe" Didrikson.

Didrikson hailed from Beaumont, Texas. Her sports career had modest beginnings. She started out as a basketball player on an insurance company team. But her amazing talent was quickly recognized. She was named all-American three times. There was almost nothing Babe couldn't do. She could swim, run, and jump better than any woman athlete before her. She played tennis, baseball, football—you name it. It would have been fine with her if they had let her enter twenty Olympic events. She was limited to only three.

Before the Olympics were over, Babe took the gold medal and set records in both the 80-meter hurdles and the javelin throw. She almost took the gold in the high jump, by jumping a record 5 feet, 5¼ inches. But she was disqualified for going over the bar head first. So Babe had to settle for a silver medal in that event. But when the Games were over, Babe had won more than her three medals. She had also won the hearts of Americans everywhere. ∎

Babe Didrikson (right) winning the 80-meter hurdles at the 1932 Olympics.

The Nazis staged a lavish show for the opening of the 1936 Olympics in Berlin.

Jesse Owens Shocks Nazis

Hitler Humiliated at Berlin Olympics

Why should we go to Berlin? This was the question Jewish and Negro athletes were asking in 1936. Berlin seemed a terrible place to hold the Olympics. Many other athletes didn't like the idea of going to Germany, either. After all, the country was headed by Nazi Adolf Hitler. Hitler's beliefs about the inferiority of Jews and Negroes were well known. In Hitler's eyes, the blond-haired, blue-eyed Germans were the strongest, smartest people in the world. They were the only people that mattered. He believed that under his leadership, the "Aryan race" would one day take over the world.

By 1936 Hitler was already trying to drive the German Jews from their country. They were not allowed in certain stores. Many Jews had their businesses and homes taken away. Hitler had also made hate-filled statements about Negroes. In his eyes, they were as bad as the Jews.

The United States Amateur Athletic Union had thought about boycotting the Games. In the end, though, they decided against it. In the summer of 1936, there were 328 U.S. athletes going to Berlin. Among them

were many American Jews and ten Negroes.

Hitler will never forget those Games. They started wonderfully. On July 21, 1936, the Olympic torch was lit at the temple of Zeus in Olympia, Greece. Three thousand runners passed the torch, day and night, across seven countries. On August 1, the last runner carried the torch into Berlin. Five thousand athletes from 53 countries watched as a smiling Hitler opened the Games.

It wasn't long before the United States athletes wiped the smile off Hitler's face. Americans took first, ⇨

second, and third place in the high jump. Cornelius Johnson won the gold medal with a new Olympic record of 6 feet, 7 5/16 inches. Dave Albritton took the silver. Both Johnson and Albritton are Negroes.

All eyes were on Hitler after the high jump event. He had shaken the hands of all the other winners that day. But those winners had all been white men. Would he shake the hands of Johnson and Albritton? Hitler left the stands in a hurry. The smile on Johnson's face told the world that he had just won a lot more than a gold medal.

But Hitler's greatest humiliation would come through the actions of another Negro, Jesse Owens. Owens was the son of Alabama sharecroppers. He was a bright young man who was studying at Ohio State University. Even before the Olympics he was known as a great athlete. In 1935 he broke three world records in a single afternoon. He ran the 220-yard dash in 20.3 seconds. He ran the 220-yard low hurdles in 22.6 seconds.

And his long jump was out of this world—26.9 feet!

Would Owens do as well in the Olympic Games? He did not disappoint himself or his United States teammates.

Owens took a record-breaking *four* gold medals. He set a new Olympic record of 10.3 seconds in the 100-meter dash. He flashed down the track in the 200-meter dash in 20.7 seconds. And a flying Owens did the long jump in 26 feet, 5½ inches. His fourth gold medal came in the 400-meter relay. In that event he and his teammates set a new world record: 39.8 seconds.

Needless to say Hitler did not congratulate Owens on any of his victories. He was nowhere to be seen while Owens was accepting his four gold medals. But that didn't really matter. The whole world had witnessed what took place in Berlin in August 1936. And people everywhere saw that Hitler's racial theories had been exposed for what they really were—nonsense. ■

Where Was Babe?

Where was Babe Didrikson at the 1936 Olympics? No doubt the United States could have used this three time medal winner. But Didrikson was barred from the 1936 Olympics by the Amateur Athletic Association. They said she lost her amateur standing when she appeared in a car ad. Look for Didrikson on the golf course. It's her latest sport.

Jesse Owens winning one of his four gold medals at the 1936 Olympics.

A Sad Farewell

His New York Yankee teammates called him the Iron Horse. Why? Lou Gehrig played in 2,130 straight games during 14 seasons with the Yankees. His lifetime batting average was a whopping .340, and he smashed 493 career home runs. Then in 1939, due to a crippling illness, Gehrig had to say goodbye to baseball. On July 4, 75,000 fans and all his former teammates turned out to honor the great first baseman. Despite what many felt was a bad break, Gehrig told the crowd, "Today, I consider myself the luckiest man on the face of the earth." ■

A saddened Lou Gehrig (left) bids farewell to baseball at a ceremony in Yankee Stadium July 4, 1939. Yankee manager Joe McCarthy (right) and opposing players share the sadness.

Joe Louis—King of the Ring

"Tonight, tonight, Joe Louis is gonna fight."

This was the excited chant of kids marching in the hot summer streets of Detroit. Indoors, people all across the country crowded around their radios, waiting to hear a blow-by-blow account of the "Brown Bomber" in action.

Joe Louis Barrow was one of the most exciting athletes of the 1930s. After only three short years as a professional, Louis won the heavyweight championship title in 1937. The 23-year-old Negro became the youngest champion ever.

Former champions like Primo Carnera, Max Baer, and Jim Braddock all fell to Joe's hammering fists. Joe's only big loss was to the German Max Schmeling. In 1936 Schmeling flattened Louis in the twelfth round with a right-hand knockout punch. But in a rematch in 1938, Louis blasted Schmeling to the canvas. The German didn't last through the first round. ■

Joe Louis (right) knocked out Max Schmeling in the first round of their rematch.

Hooray for Hollywood!

The 1930s were troubled times. After all, there was a lot to be unhappy about. How did people have fun during these difficult times? How in the world did they keep a smile on their faces?

Some went out and played the new game of "miniature" golf. Others stayed home, listened to the radio, and did puzzles. But for millions of Americans the local movie theater provided the best cure for the Depression blues.

There were many reasons why people flocked to the movies during the 1930s. One reason was that Hollywood came up with a perfect idea for the economic hard times: the double feature. For 25 cents, audiences could see two full-length movies in one sitting. With many Americans hard up for money, an entertainment bargain like this was hard to resist.

Of course there were dozens and dozens of other reasons people fell in love with the movies. They wanted to see the glamorous movie stars who filled the screens in memorable movies. Handsome leading men like Clark Gable, Cary Grant, Spencer Tracy, and Errol Flynn made female movie fans dreamy-eyed. Beautiful actresses like Jean Harlow, Greta Garbo, Joan Crawford, and Katherine Hepburn did the same for men.

Many new stars became popular during the decade. There were child stars (dimple-faced, curly-haired Shirley Temple). There were athletic stars (former Olympic swimmer Johnny Weismuller playing Tarzan).

James Cagney played a streetwise gangster in the movie *The Public Enemy*. Blonde "bombshell" Jean Harlow played his girlfriend.

There were even monster ("Franken-stein") and gorilla ("King Kong") stars.

Hollywood turned out movies for just about everyone's taste in the '30s. Comedies—with the Marx Brothers, Laurel and Hardy, and W. C. Fields—made people laugh and forget their troubles. Action films like "Mutiny on the Bounty" and "The Adventures of Robin Hood" gave audiences the chance to escape to another place and time. And musicals—many starring the great dance team of Fred Astaire and Ginger Rogers—made many people feel like dancing themselves.

Hollywood also took notice of the stories coming right from the decade's newspaper headlines. Every day people could read about real-life hoodlums like Al Capone, John Dillinger, and "Pretty Boy" Floyd. Then in the evening they could see silver screen gangsters like James Cagney, Edward G. Robinson, and Humphrey Bogart imitating their real-life counterparts. In the movies, as in real life, the bad guys usually lost. ⇨

The silver screen's premier dance couple: Fred Astaire and Ginger Rogers.

In 1933, movie audiences were thrilled and chilled by the Hollywood production, _King Kong_.

Was there any one movie from the '30s that audiences loved above all others? Many people would say it was David O. Selznik's *Gone With the Wind*. The movie was filmed in full color—a new technique Hollywood introduced in the mid-1930s. And it starred the popular and handsome Clark Gable and a beautiful new-comer named Vivien Leigh.

An epic story of the Civil War, *Gone With the Wind* was filled with many memorable scenes. But one line summed up the feelings of many Americans during the Depression. It was spoken by Scarlet O'Hara (Miss Leigh). Faced with her plantation in ruins, and no money or means of support, she dramatically vows to " . . . never go hungry again." It was a vow many depression-weary people could well understand. ■

Clark Gable and Vivien Leigh starred in Hollywood's epic Civil War drama, *Gone With the Wind*.

The Hoax of the Decade

It is the night of October 30, 1938. Millions of Americans cannot believe what they hear on the radio. Martians, armed with death rays, have landed near Princeton, New Jersey. Though a voice on the radio says to stay calm, the country panics. In Newark, more than twenty families run from their homes. They cover their faces with wet towels to shield themselves from the deadly Martian gas. Two university professors set out to find the Martian landing spot. Thousands of New Yorkers run to parks, looking for safety. People from coast to coast gather eagerly around their radios, listening for their fates.

Later, these Martian-fearing folks were surprised to find out that they had missed a very important

Orson Welles's Halloween eve broadcast about a "Martian invasion" frightened thousands of Americans.

announcement: "The Columbia Broadcasting System . . . presents Orson Welles and the Mercury Theater of the Air in *The War of the Worlds* by H. G. Wells." The Martians were pure imagination, an adaptation of the Wells's story set in the present-day United States. The radio show was only entertainment—a Halloween "trick or treat" for America.

But much of America was not amused. When they learned the truth, thousands of people angrily protested to CBS about the broadcast. A few people even threatened to kill the show's creator, Orson Welles!

But feelings were soothed when CBS and Welles issued an apology. And no real harm came from the broadcast, except for the distress of a few very frightened citizens. The show did, however, prove the power and influence of the small box that millions of people had in their homes: the radio. ■

Eugene O'Neill

The Dark Side of a Great Playwright

His name is Eugene O'Neill. His face may not be famous, but his words are. In 1936 he won the Nobel Prize for literature—a well-deserved reward for this great American writer. In the past 20 years he had given the world 25 plays, many of them memorable. But everyone who has seen O'Neill's plays knows that he is both brilliant and haunted. What is behind this man and his work?

Eugene O'Neill was born in New York City on October 16, 1888. His father, James O'Neill, was a famous Irish-born actor. His mother, Ella, was Irish-American. The playwright had one older brother, James.

While still in his early teens, Eugene discovered a terrible secret about his mother. She was a drug addict, in constant need of the pain-killer, morphine. Ella O'Neill had first been given the drug by her doctor. It was used to treat the pain she experienced during and after Eugene's birth. Some say that to this day, O'Neill somehow blames himself for his mother's sickness.

Like his brother, James, Eugene O'Neill became a heavy drinker. After a year at Princeton, he dropped out and went to sea. When he returned, he married a beautiful woman named Kathleen Jenkins. But he didn't remain with her long. A restless man, he soon left the country to look for gold in Honduras. While he was gone, his first son was born. Kathleen divorced O'Neill. The wandering father did not meet his son until the boy was 11 years old.

O'Neill's hard life style caught up with him in 1912. In poor health, he spent six months in a hospital. During this time O'Neill thought a lot about his future. He decided to become a playwright.

He spent a year at Harvard, learning the art of playwriting. Soon his plays began to entertain and shock America. In *All God's Chillun Got Wings*, O'Neill tells the story of a Negro man and a white woman who fall in love and marry. They fight not only the racism of the world, but racism within themselves. Nothing like it had ever been seen on the American stage before.

Some of O'Neill's other plays, show the dark side of family life. In *Desire Under the Elms*, a woman kills her child to prove her love for a man.

O'Neill has also brought a different look to the American theatre. Masks, music, and dance add life and meaning to many of his plays.

Many theatergoers find O'Neill's plays dark and uncomfortable, much like the writer's life. But they leave the theater knowing why he won the Nobel Prize. ∎

Nobel Prize winning author Eugene O'Neill

Franklin D. Roosevelt
A Confident, Courageous President

The year was 1887. Little Franklin Roosevelt, five years old, found himself in the White House. His father had brought him to meet Grover Cleveland, president of the United States. President Cleveland looked down at the young Roosevelt and his blond curls. "My little man," he said, "I am making a strange wish for you. It is that you will never be president of the United States."

What would Grover think now? The little boy has not only grown up to be president—but some say the greatest president since Abraham Lincoln. What do we know of the life of this man everyone calls FDR?

Franklin Delano Roosevelt was born to James and Sara Roosevelt on January 30, 1882, in Hyde Park, New York. He was their only son, and some would say he was spoiled. James Roosevelt, a wealthy businessman, gave Franklin everything a boy could want—horses to ride, boats to sail, and guns to shoot. And Sara was a doting mother. She guarded the young boy jealously.

When he was 14, Franklin went to boarding school in Boston. Later he went on to Harvard. He was not seen as an outstanding student. But he passed all his courses, and then went on to practice law. Later, Roosevelt would say that he never found his place in life until he went into politics. Franklin, of course, was not the first Roosevelt to hold office. His cousin, Theodore Roosevelt, had served as the United States president from 1901 to 1909.

In 1905 Franklin married his fifth cousin, Eleanor. Their life together was normal and happy enough, until 1921. Then Roosevelt was struck with polio while at his summer home in Campobello. His legs would never again carry him without braces. To this day, he continues to vacation in Warm Springs, Georgia. There he swims with other victims of polio, working toward rehabilitation.

But Americans do not think of Roosevelt in terms of his crippled legs. They think of him as an inspiring, courageous leader. They think of him as a confident voice on the radio, comforting the nation in his "fireside chats." They think of him as "Mr. New Deal," a source of hope to the many poor and homeless. These are the accomplishments that have made him newsmaker of the decade. ∎

A young Franklin Roosevelt campaigns for the New York Senate in 1910.

FDR's Political Life to 1940

1910: Elected to New York state senate.

1912: Re-elected to New York state senate.

1913: Appointed assistant secretary of the Navy; served until 1920.

1920: Unsuccessful candidate for vice president on Democratic ticket with James Cox.

1928: Elected governor of New York.

1930: Re-elected governor of New York.

1932: Elected president of the United States.

1936: Re-elected president of the United States.

Nobel Peace Prize

Jane Addams

More than twenty years ago, some people in the United States said that Jane Addams was un-American. They didn't like it when she spoke out as founder of the Women's International League for Peace and Freedom. After all, she dared to suggest that the United States stay clear of war! That was an unpopular idea in 1917. Today, many of those same Americans see the wisdom in her suggestion. In 1931 Addams's lifelong work for peace—and for the poor—was rewarded with the Nobel Peace Prize.

Addams is known best for founding Chicago's Hull House in 1889. In that settlement house, down-and-out people could find shelter and support. That help was provided by Addams and her partner, Ellen Gates Starr.

But Hull House was just the beginning of a larger movement for better living and working conditions. Addams and her friends also worked to improve the bad neighborhood around Hull House. From there, they campaigned to improve housing and public welfare.

In 1911 Addams published "Twenty Years at Hull House." The book told of the hardships and triumphs of running the settlement house.

Born in 1860 to a wealthy Illinois family, Addams went to school at Rockford Seminary. In the late 1880s, she went through a number of painful operations on her back. Her family sent her to Europe to recover.

While in Spain, Addams first had the idea of starting a settlement house for the poor. She dreamed that it would be a place for unfortunate people to get back on their feet.

Before returning to America, she went to England to visit Toynbee Hall, a famous settlement house in London. A year later, she opened Hull House.

Throughout her life, Addams believed strongly in the need for research into the causes of poverty and crime. She stressed the importance of training social workers to help the poor and of organizing groups to bring pressure on government officials.

Addams's efforts helped get many laws passed benefiting working women and children, and those living in terrible housing conditions.

Jane Addams died in 1935. ∎

Jane Addams spent her life trying to help the underprivileged.

The Louisiana Kingfish

Huey Long

His name was Huey Long. But to the people of the South, he was known simply as the "Kingfish." Huey Long had ambitions. He wanted to be president of the United States. And the Kingfish might have made it—if a bullet hadn't stopped him.

Huey Long was born in 1893. He was the eighth of nine children. The son of a poor couple, he lived his early years in a four-room log cabin. On hot summer days, he worked in the fields by his parent's side. The Longs were poor, but young Huey wasn't planning to stay that way.

Long never questioned what he would do in life. He wanted to be in public office. At the age of only 24, he became Louisiana's railroad commissioner. In that job he made enemies when he headed a fight against Standard Oil. Long believed other small oil companies should be allowed to use Standard's pipelines. It was a long court fight, and Standard Oil lost. Small businesses in Louisiana cheered Huey Long. At last they had someone on their side.

Then in 1924, Long ran for governor. He made a name for himself as he traveled the countryside in search of votes. Some people said he sounded more like a preacher than a politician. In a singsong voice, he promised good roads, good schools, and free schoolbooks for children. He telephoned farmers at night and asked for their votes. Louisiana's poor, both white and Negro, began to take a liking to this red-headed, big-nosed man. He was saying what they wanted to hear. But on election day, rain ruined Long's chance to be governor. Many poor farmers could not travel the muddy roads to reach the polls. Long lost by only 11,000 votes.

He didn't give up. Four years later he ran again. People all across the state came to know his favorite saying, "Every man a king, but no man wears a crown." Election day in 1928 was a clear, dry day. The farmers got out to vote. And Long became the new governor of Louisiana.

It's hard to say whether Long was a good or bad governor. On one hand, he was a bully. He fired all state workers who did not support him. State police were ordered to beat up important business leaders who fought him. And government officials were bribed to see things

Louisiana's Kingfish, Huey Long

his way. Louisiana belonged to the Kingfish, and he let no one get in his way.

On the other hand, farmers got their roads and bridges. Medical clinics appeared in the poorest parts of the state. Louisiana State University got a new medical school. And children got their free schoolbooks—all because of Governor Huey "Kingfish" Long.

In 1930 Long won a seat in the United States Senate. Two years later he helped to elect Franklin Roosevelt, because he believed in Roosevelt's New Deal. But once FDR was in office, Long changed his mind. He found that he could not get FDR to do things his way. So Long went on the warpath. His plan was to win the presidency from "Prince Franklin" in 1936.

The rest of America didn't know what to make of the campaigning Kingfish. Here was a man, dressed in a fancy white suit and wearing diamond rings. And he was talking about improving the lives of the poor! His "Share Our Wealth" program was astounding. It would limit a person's yearly income to $1,800,000. Under Long's plan no one in America could be worth more than $5 million. Each person, he believed, should be guaranteed earnings of $2,500 a year. Schooling, from kindergarten through college, would be free to all. The government would sell food at a low price to the poor. All would share in the riches of America. That was Long's dream.

But the Kingfish had made too many enemies. One of them was Dr. Carl Weiss. On September 8, 1935, Weiss shot a single, well-aimed bullet into the stomach of Huey Long and killed him. In turn, Long's bodyguards shot Weiss more than 60 times and killed him. Huey Long's dream for himself—and America—had ended in a nightmare. ■

Amelia Earhart

Climbing to Great Heights
Amelia Earhart

In 1918 young Amelia Earhart was living and working in Toronto, Canada. It was her job to care for soldiers wounded in the War in Europe. It was hard, depressing work. Day in and day out she saw pain, wasted youth, and broken dreams.

Then one day, her friend Captain Spaulding took Earhart to a nearby airfield. As she watched the planes take off into the cold winter clouds, her own dream was born. Perhaps she was attracted to the freedom of the sky. Or perhaps she saw the sky as a place with no pain. All Earhart knew was that she wanted to fly. And fly she did.

In 1920 she signed up for flying lessons in Los Angeles, California. Two crash landings didn't stop her from getting her license. For a time, her parents and sister tried to talk her out of flying. But they knew they didn't have much hope.

Amelia's family watched her grow up in Kansas City. In those days the lively girl climbed fences, and explored the countryside around her home. Her family knew Amelia was a pioneer, just as her grandparents had been when they crossed the plains. Finally her family gave in, and on Amelia's 24th birthday, they bought her a small yellow biplane, a Kinner Canary.

Earhart didn't waste any time. In 1922 she broke the women's record for altitude, flying the little plane to a dangerous height of 14,000 feet.

In 1928, Earhart was invited to be the first woman to fly across the Atlantic. She couldn't resist the challenge, even though she was only allowed to be a passenger. The flight was a success. But Earhart vowed that someday she would fly the Atlantic on her own.

Her chance came on May 20, 1932. Then the daring thirty-four-year-old woman set off from New Brunswick, Canada, carrying only some soup and tomato juice. At one point, ice on the plane's wings and thick fog nearly plunged her into the gray Atlantic. But fifteen hours later, with her small plane almost out of gas, she landed on a field in Ireland. "I've come from America," she said to the farmer who greeted her. Her smile was as wide as the sky she had just crossed.

Earhart continued to make history in the years to come. Twice she broke the women's speed record for a flight from Los Angeles to New York. In 1935 she became the first person, man or woman, to fly from Hawaii to California.

On June 1, 1937, Earhart began her grandest flight ever. She and her navigator, Frank Noonan, took off from Miami. They planned to circle the world, flying close to the equator all the way.

Earhart and Noonan flew more than 22,000 miles. But then, with less than 7,000 miles to go, their plane disappeared over the Pacific Ocean. Not even the United States Navy could find any trace of the plane or the passengers. Amelia Earhart, one of America's true, modern-day pioneers, was lost to her beloved sky. ∎

GLOSSARY

abdication: when a king or queen gives up the throne.

Abraham Lincoln Brigade: a group of men and women from the United States who went to Spain to help the Loyalists in the Spanish Civil War.

anarchist: a person who wants to live with no official system of government or any other authorities.

anti-semitism: the practice of hating Jewish people simply because they are Jewish.

Aryan: Hitler's name for what he considered the "true" and "pure" German people.

civil war: a war between different groups of people within the same country.

depression: a period in which there is very high unemployment and a financial crisis that makes it hard to create jobs.

Dust Bowl: the name given to the part of the western and southwestern United States devastated by dust storms in the 1930s.

fireside chats: radio talks by President Franklin D. Roosevelt that informed and reassured the nation.

Kristallnacht: a German term, meaning literally "The Night of [Breaking] Crystal," for November 9, 1938, when Germans burned Jewish synagogues and began to openly persecute Jews.

musicals: movies in which the plot is built around song-and-dance numbers.

Nazis: extremely nationalistic, anti-semitic Germans who followed the leadership of Adolf Hitler between the years 1933 and 1945.

New Deal: a combination of programs introduced in 1933 by U.S. President Franklin D. Roosevelt to create jobs for Americans and end the Great Depression.

Prohibition: a period in the United States when Americans were legally prevented from making or selling alcoholic beverages.

Scottsboro Boys: nine young African-American men unjustly accused of rape in Alabama in 1931.

WPA: the Works Progress Administration, a U.S. government agency set up to employ artists during the Great Depression.

BOOKS FOR FURTHER READING

The titles listed below provide more detailed information about some of the people and events described in this book. Ask for them at your local library or bookstore.

A Child's Diary — The 1930s. Johnson (Wishing Room)

The Abraham Lincoln Brigade: Americans Fighting Fascism in the Spanish Civil War. Lawson (HarperCollins Children's Books)

Amelia Earhart — Charles Lindbergh. Farr and Fago (Pendulum Press)

The Great Depression and the New Deal: America's Economic Collapse and Recovery. Scharff (Franklin Watts)

Franklin D. Roosevelt and the New Deal. Shebar (Barron)

Portrait of a Decade: Nineteen Thirties. Freeman (Trafalgar Square)

PLACES TO WRITE OR VISIT

Franklin D. Roosevelt Library
and Museum
511 Albany Post Road
Hyde Park, NY 12538

Museum of the Cinema
360 McGill Street
Montreal, Quebec H2Y 2E9

The Smithsonian Institution
1000 Jefferson Drive S.W.
Washington, D.C. 20560

INDEX